W9-AGZ-430

THE UFFDA TRIAL

Gerald Anderson

MARTIN HOUSE PUBLICATIONS
Hastings, MN 55033

MARTIN HOUSE PUBLICATIONS
BOX 274
HASTINGS, MN 55033

Printed in the United States of America

Published by Martin House Publications
Box 274, Hastings, MN 55033

Library of Congress Catalog Card Number 93-080440

ISBN 0-9613437-3-7

Second Printing

Illustrated by Barbara Anderson
Edited by Suzann Nelson and Julie Stockman
Cover designed by Lisa Beytien-Carlson
Cover Photo courtesy of *Minnesota Historical Society*,
Clay County Court House MC6.9/MH8/r2

**In memory of Wilferd,
my Dad, 1903 - 1985**

Contents

1

The Threshing Crew

1

Mrs. Haugen had never made a better threshing dinner. The steak had been cooked a couple hours longer than necessary, and had virtually suffocated in the greasy tomato sauce.

In other parts of the country it would have been called *Swiss steak*. Mrs. Haugen had called it "steak in red sauce." No one ever argued with that name. Besides, it wasn't *half-bad* sauce, and after one had dribbled it over boiled potatoes, it could really be appreciated. The thirteen men in the threshing crew had gone through eight of the eleven pounds of steak that Mrs. Haugen had served up and might have gone through more, had it not been for the sausage which she managed to serve at every meal. Two loaves of incredibly heavy and coarse bread had also disappeared washed down with several pots of coffee. Vegetables were never a popular choice, but everybody took some just to be polite. That day it was green peas in cream sauce. The day before it had been green peas in cream sauce and, near as anyone could remember, it had been green peas in cream sauce the day before that. Peas went well with chicken, steak and roast pork and since that was all anybody ever served at threshing meals, it was accepted.

There were also pickles. Of all the women who served the threshing crew, Mrs. Haugen served the worst pickles. Other people's pickles were a comforting and soothing shade of green with regular little bumps on them, but Mrs. Haugen's pickles were an offensive light green with an occasional streak of almost pure white. Everybody took one so as not to offend her, but rather than savoring them as one did with Mrs. Iverson's pickles, one tried to eat them as quickly as possible. Another tactic was to eat them with another mouthful of food hoping that it would somehow ameliorate the nasty vinegar taste. They even looked suspicious. Even the bumps were irregular; they seemed to have been worn down by something. It was with a certain measure of delight that many members of the crew discovered that the red sauce could not only conceal the color of the pickles, but could even partially subdue the nastiness.

No one talked much during the meal. Aside from an occasional, "Yesus, it's hot" delivered when Mrs. Haugen was safely in the kitchen, most of the conversation consisted of "pass the...", thank you, and grunts. Eating was serious business because the threshing crew burned calories at the same rate as a gang of Swedish lumberjacks. Besides, the sooner one got through the main meal, the sooner one could lay into the pie. Pie was, like peas, one of the more reliable expectations for the threshers' dinner but, unlike the peas, it came in a greater variety.

In the past week, in fact, the crew had gone through three different hostesses and seven kinds of pie. These had ranged from the terrific (the sour cream raisin), through the great (the apple and blueberry), the pretty good (the rhubarb and cherry), and the not bad (a runny banana cream), to the awful (a lemon meringue). Mrs. Haugen usually tempted everyone with a Juneberry pie, an apple pie, and a pumpkin pie. The sooner one finished, the sooner one could choose pie. At Mrs. Haugen's table it usually meant that six out of the first seven people who were asked would take the apple. Since the pie was always cut into six pieces, that choice was gone in a hurry. The next five people, forewarned by tradition, virtually always took the pumpkin pie, and the last two luckless and slothful eaters were faced with the Juneberry.

After another cup of coffee or so, each diner mumbled something complimentary to a blushing Mrs. Haugen, and went outside to lie on the grass under a tree. This, too, was traditional; sort of an old world Scandinavian siesta to aid digestion and to rest. And, let it also be said, threshers did earn their rest. Some would close their eyes and nap for twenty minutes, some would smoke, and some would swap dirty jokes or observations about the weather.

Occasionally they would belch or break wind with an equal degree of satisfaction, usually followed by an expression of disgust from the others.

Paul Thorson, in fact, had just produced such reports on Mrs. Haugen's dinner when his brother Karl said, "That's what it's all about for you, isn't it?"

"Huh?" said the startled Paul.

"I mean, the thing of it is, you can accept this without questioning it at all. How many years have we been on this threshing crew? How many years are we going to be on it? Have we advanced one single step in life since we started doing this? I'm twenty-three years old and I'm still the older Thorson boy. You should be the younger Thorson boy, but you never are. Why? Why is that?"

"I don't know," Paul admitted, wiping his glasses on his omnipresent shirt tail, "but now that you mention it, I guess you're right. Maybe it's because you are always questioning things and reading about things to the point where people get a little bit suspicious of you. It is considered bad form to break out of mediocrity."

"I notice you've never been tempted."

"Is that fair? Look. Here we are at the dinner table. Everybody else is just trying to choke down their food, but not you. No, you have to inform everyone that in England they don't call corn 'corn' like we do. There, the term corn is used in a generic sense, essentially the same way we would say grain. First of all, nobody at the table gives a damn what they call corn in England and second of all, I'm probably the only other person there who knows what 'generic' means, and I'm not really that sure that I do."

Karl, becoming animated to the point of rising up from the grass to lean on his elbows, protested, "Dad knew what it meant and he thought it was interesting."

"Well maybe, but Ingvald sneered."

"Ah, I see I am to conduct myself for the approval of Ingvald Johnson," said Karl, as he crossed his hands behind his head and stretched out on the thick green grass.

In another ten minutes they would be on their way out to the field again. Karl looked over the farm that spread around him. Bjørn Haugen kept a nice place, he thought. The house was white, of course, and surrounded by a nice grove of box elders. It was on a slight hill so that, even though it was very hot, there was a breeze that both cooled and kept the mosquitoes away. Bjørn had even contrived to make a little street in a straight downward slope to the main road between his buildings. On one side there was a "machineshedwoodshedgarage", a grainery, and a chicken coop. On the other side of the *street* was the barn which was a careful transplant from Norway. It was, as all the other outbuildings, red with white trim. Just as Norwegian barns had taken advantage of the mountainside, Bjørn had taken advantage of whatever hill he could find. The barn was three stories tall with a ramp and a little bridge allowing a tractor or a team of horses to go directly into the second floor. On the first floor, which could be entered from the rear, one could keep a manure spreader. On the third floor was the hay mow. In short, it was a farm version of Henry Ford's assembly line; the hay went from the hay mow to the second floor where it went through the cow and from there on down to the first floor. Karl wished that his father had a barn like that.

Paul, meanwhile, knew what kind of mood his brother was working himself into. Moreover, he liked when Karl got that way; he was more fun to talk to. Paul never took things as seriously as Karl did, partly because he didn't have to assume any real responsibility for the farm. He had long made known his determination to leave the farm as soon as possible, and everybody accepted that. Karl, for all his bookishness, loved the land. Paul had a feeling that this would be his last time as a member of the threshing crew, and he was glad.

Paul was about the same size as Karl, but looked more ethnic. He had blonde hair and blue eyes and looked like a refugee off a Norwegian sardine boat. He was quite nearsighted and wore thick wire-rimmed glasses that curled around his ears. Individually described, his features should have made him more handsome than Karl, but he wasn't--perhaps because his nose was too straight.

Karl had suffered through a childhood of being called "that

nice looking boy," and was now a nice looking man. With light brown hair that achieved an almost neutral color in the summer sun, he was darker than Paul. He had eyes that were a composite of warm brown and glittering bits of green, the kind of eyes that people used to call hazel. He did not have a face of perfect symmetry, however. His nose took a slight turn to the left. If you were not looking for it, you wouldn't have noticed but it was the first thing Karl saw when he looked in the mirror. His brother, Paul, only made it worse by claiming that Karl was the only man in Minnesota whose eyes focused on the same side of his nose.

Karl sometimes regretted that he didn't live in a mansion on the East Coast, where Jay Gatsby and friends might drop by and commiserate with him over the unfortunate polo accident that had resulted in his broken nose. Or maybe, if he had gone to the University of Minnesota, he could have claimed that he broke his nose in the big Illinois game while tackling Red Grange. If he were only a little older, he might have been able to convince people that he had broken his nose in action in the Argonne forest.

Unfortunately, everybody in the Vingelen area already knew the truth. He had broken his nose on a pig. Pa had told Karl and Paul to castrate five little pigs. Neither Karl nor Paul knew how to do this (except, of course, as a general principle) and so they delayed it. They delayed until the little pigs were no longer very little. Pa, who could see no need to have five more boars on the farm, finally agreed to show them. Pa would do the actual surgery with a barber's razor while Karl and Paul--each holding a hind leg--would immobilize the patient. But the pig was understandably reluctant to part with his future fatherhood, and there were no anesthesiologists to relax him. As Pa began the incision on the first would-be sire, Paul, perhaps out of sympathy for the unfortunate swine, lost his grip. This caused Karl to lose his balance, slip on pig manure, and, in the finest tradition of wrestling flips, bring the pig down upon his nose. Blood, both human and porcine, reddened the straw. Pa and Karl, who rarely cussed, now openly swore while Paul, who frequently cussed, now laughed. It had hurt, of course, but Karl didn't think it was broken and didn't want the story to get around. His strategy was wrong on both counts;

the nose was broken, and everyone soon knew the circumstances. Ironically, Pa and Paul both lived up to their vows of silence, but Ma went to Ladies Aid that very afternoon and brought back all sorts of condolences for Karl.

Still, Karl was a nice looking man, the best looking of the brothers. He was clean shaven now, but thought he just might grow another beard in the winter. Actually, he did not really look good in a beard but he liked to grow one anyway because it was out of fashion. Karl was an independent man.

At length, Karl gave out with a mournful sigh. "The thing is, you know, that people should find it interesting that they use the word 'corn' for 'grain' in England. They should sit back and immediately ask 'why is that?' It should engender a dinnertime conversation about the way language changes, or at least a derogatory comment about the English. I think Pa would have said something but he had his mouth full, and I've long since learned not to count on you."

"You know the bottom line of your attempt to start a conversation, don't you? You were one of the poor saps who had to have the Juneberry pie," Paul laughed, totally without sympathy.

Karl nodded in resignation. "Under ordinary circumstances that might have been a small price to pay, but to tell you the truth, it was especially awful today. Next time--if ever there is one--try to help me out. You could have asked Bjørn what they called corn in Norway for instance."

"What do I care what they call corn in Norway?"

"Once again you show an acute perception of how to get along in the world. It's always been that way. I had to wait until I was eight years old before I could sit on the pony. The moment I got up there Ma said, `It's not fair that only Karl should ride the pony. Let Paul ride him too.' The day I got to drive Pa's car, you got to drive Pa's car. I've always been one and a half years older than you, but you have always been one and a half years ahead of me. I know that doesn't make sense, but you know what I mean. Now you're seen as one heck of a regular guy who's a full-fledged member of the threshing crew, and I'm still seen as the 'older Thorson boy.' Go along, don't question, and nod in agreement at the most inane observations. I don't think I have ever heard anyone say 'yah, it sure is hot' with the conviction that you bring to the average conversation."

Paul wiped his glasses, scratched himself, pulled up his socks, and wiped his glasses some more before he said with a deliberate attempt to be tactful, "Well, Karl, it's your own damn fault. When somebody tells you 'it sure is hot', you don't have to remind them that it's always hot this time of the year because of the position of the earth in relation to the sun. Who cares? All anybody expects from you is a 'yah, it sure is'."

Karl scowled in recognition of the unpleasant truth. "I know, Paul. You're right. I guess part of it is that I just need to decide who I want to be. You do the black land farmer routine so well that it seems unfair that you want to leave it and I want to stay. But I like to plan. I like to consider other alternatives, and I like to develop well thought out contingencies. Even as I was eating that horrible pickle of Mrs. Haugen's I was thinking about how I could avoid it next time. By the way, what are you burying in the grass?"

"Huh? Oh, well, I have my own ways of dealing with Mrs. Haugen's pickles," said Paul, as he straightened up and kicked more grass over his pickle tomb. It was time to go back out in the field. "You going into Vingelen tonight?"

Karl hesitated but then said, "Yah, I s'pose I will. Nothing ever happens in that town, but if I don't go, who will keep an eye on you?" He reached up and peeled some box elder leaves off a tree and loosely packed them in his straw hat. "Nature's cooling system," he explained to Paul, who declined to follow his brother's example.

2

Vingelen,
A Scandinavian
Community

2

The residents of Vingelen, who were the defendants in the great Minnesota Uffda Trial, were as American as baseball, apple pie, and *lutefisk*. Unlike their parents, they spoke American almost all the time. They were second and even third generation *Scandahoovians*, and Minnesota was New Scandinavia.

Scandinavian senators and representatives had gone to Washington and in 1926, Governor Christianson was one of in an unbroken line of Scandinavians who would occupy the governor's chair for seventy years. It was a dry America and a Minnesota congressman, Representative Andrew Volstead, had helped make it that way. A song of the time recognized this, observing:

"Ten thousand Jews were peddling booze without the
state's permission, to fill the needs of a million Swedes
who voted for prohibition."

In August, the Red River Valley may have reminded some of the old immigrants of the fields of southern Sweden, but the younger farmers didn't care. Their grandparents had tried to live on a few acres and now they, the younger ones, were farming a full quarter section. They had a few chickens, a few pigs, a few cows, and at least one team of horses. A few farms even had a couple of goats to provide the raw material for *geitost*, the tasty goat cheese. The real money, however, was to be made in wheat, barley, or potatoes. At least, it should have been.

The booming economy of the Roaring Twenties never quite trickled down to the farmers. They had prospered during the Great War though, and even if they weren't showing much of a profit for a year's labor, they somehow felt secure in their future. There has never been a successful farmer who was not an optimist. As Wall Street was bullish, so was the farm yard and, after all, one didn't get a newborn calf on the margin.

Vingelen, Minnesota, where two tall grain elevators dominated and constituted the skyline, was a focal point of local farming activities. The town was named after a little community in Norway and appeared, to any impartial observer, to have been a literal transplant. It had a weekly newspaper printed partly in English, and partly in Norwegian. The **Vingelen Standard** could also have been printed in Swedish, but the editor was Norwegian and reasoned, correctly enough, that although the Swedes wouldn't always admit it, they could read Norwegian about as well as Swedish, and a whole lot better than English.

There were three competing general stores all selling about the same thing for the same price, and none of them prospering. Before prohibition, two saloons had stood on opposite ends of Main Street and everyone in town knew who went into which saloon and how often they did so. They were cafes now, but the traditional patronage remained. The Vingelen Hotel--with its broad porch, clean rooms, and low rates--attracted traveling salesmen and visitors from such exotic places as Fargo and Grand Forks. Prominently displayed in the drab lobby were postcards that featured the nearby Rose Gardens (unfortunately, in black and white only). Two hardware stores, a large creamery, a hatchery, a theater, a new three-story consolidated school, a blacksmith shop, a modern railroad depot, and a few dozen houses with large porches completed Vingelen's bid to become one of the country's (or at least the county's) great cities.

There were a few more Norwegians than Swedes, but most newcomers wouldn't be able to tell the difference. Most of the young people could speak both languages and often didn't realize that what they actually spoke was a curious hybrid tongue of Swedish idioms placed in a Norwegian format.

There was one German family that had somehow managed to penetrate this American Scandinavia. They did their typical German farming three miles south of town and had been somewhat outside the general circle of the community in the years before the Great War, but when America went to war, they took down the picture of the Kaiser and let everyone know whose side they were on. Of course, the fact that the Schmidt boys were the best basketball players the town could field probably had something to do with the German family's general acceptance. There was nothing else to blemish the township rolls which read like a page out of the Oslo directory--no poverty, no particular brilliance, and no crime could be found in Vingelen. No crime, that is, until the events of the Uffda Trial unfolded.

To be young in 1926 meant knowing every bootlegger in the area, whether or not one ever did business with him. It meant knowing that every part in your Model T would fit into your neighbor's Model T and, more important, that his would fit into yours. It meant an unspoken obligation to work hard in the fields, but an equally important obligation to be in town on Saturday night.

On any given Saturday night in the summer, the population would double from its customary two hundred and fifty inhabitants. The old world's "*Åssen går det*?" ("How goes it?") would be met by the fractured but all important question of the new; "Vell, are yew in town tew?" The cafe on the corner, popular for its two huge pool tables and magazine rack, would not seat everyone so the young people stood, and the older men gathered outside on the steps to talk, nod, and spit *snus*. After the relative merits of the crops and weather had been thoroughly ruminated upon, a long pause would follow, broken only by an occasional "yah", delivered in a long wheezy expulsion. The definitive "yah" was more often than not followed by an equally out-of-place, "no", as the men ponderously rose to seek members of their family who might be interested in going home.

By this time, the women of the family had done their shopping at one of the stores, had exhausted the topics of children and weather, and had once again repeated the gossip that had been heard in town last Saturday night. The needed groceries were placed in the Model T, and the week was brought to its traditional close. The grocery bag held mostly staples but, if times looked a little better, an occasional bag of *boughten* cookies was included "yust to have on hand."

The young drove their cars, or somebody else's cars, in search of a dance. If they had enough gas, it was not unusual to find them in Orebro, Ulven, Holm or any of a half dozen villages no different from Vingelen. There the *orchestra*, consisting mainly of accordions and drums, would offer up a steady stream of schottisches which sounded exactly the same to all but the most discerning ear. The waltzes and polkas had somewhat more variation, but were often indistinguishable to those dancers who took the same steps no matter what the music. An hour after the dance began, it was impossible to see across the dance hall because of the dust. The dance halls were not the cleanest places to begin with, and the inevitable sawdust or corn meal sprinkled on the floor did not exactly improve the atmosphere.

The bootleggers always did their best business on the perimeter of such happenings, and it was always a matter of record that those from out of town seemed to do much more drinking than did the natives of the community. This observation held true in all the neighboring towns however, so it was a constant source of amazement that "those who were *full*" always came from somewhere else.

The more sedate revelers could always retire to the sanctity of their own homes to tune in a new radio. Station WDAY in Fargo, North Dakota, had been broadcasting for some time, and many listeners were able to receive more distant broadcasts. The East Coast culture of Moh Jong, Flappers 23 Skiddo, Babe Ruth, and speakeazys, was a long way off, but most were aware of it. They also were aware that Sinclair Lewis' Main Street concerned a town only about one hundred miles away, and they smarted under the constant abuse poured upon them by H.L. Mencken who knew little and cared less about their problems. The Americans portrayed by another Minnesotan, F. Scott Fitzgerald, were far more foreign to them than the Norwegians in the novels of O. E. Rolvaag. On Saturday nights, the sons of the Giants of the Earth finished one week and were about to begin another in the twin repositories of their culture--the barn and the church, respectively.

16

Cows, as every farmer knows, do not give milk. One has to take it from them. And whether or not the dance had lasted far into the night, the ritual of morning chores had to be observed. To make matters worse, the chores had to be done early, for one had to go to church if for no other reason than to see who didn't. It was a habit. It was a tradition, but it was far more. Even though members of the two churches in town, and the half dozen in the country, would often avoid each other, the congregations themselves were still bound by that "faith of their fathers."

The Swedish church was out in the country. In town there were two Norwegian churches, both Lutheran but attached to rival synods: "Hauge's Synod" and the "High Church." The two churches were just across the road from each other, and both were flanked by rows of large and gaudy granite monuments memorializing those immigrants who had made it all possible, but who had never been comfortable with the fact that *that other church* was located so near to their resting places. Most of the young were not sure why the other church (whichever one it referred to) was to be treated with such suspicion, but one church closed the Lord's Prayer with "forever. Amen," and the other tried to find favor through verbosity by saying "forever and ever. Amen." Clearly God would ultimately prefer one or the other.

The two churches in Vingelen held services at the same time and this was beginning to create genuine parking problems. Most distressing, perhaps, was the fact that the gravestones took all the best parking places and it was frequently regretted that the founders of the church hadn't at least thought of that. One of the churches conducted an English language service once a month now, although the other church still assumed it was sinful to do so even though they did admit that attendance was always greater at the English service. Perhaps God had emigrated too, for it was now generally accepted that He had learned English.

No doubt about it, Vingelen was changing and most of the young thought it was for the better. Only fifty-five years had passed since Sten Hansson, a Swede, became the first white occupant of these prairies. His farm cabin had served as the stopover point for scores of immigrants migrating from the earlier

Norwegian settlements in such places as Decorah, Iowa. Now it had become a real village with a telephone system, a light plant, and newly graveled streets. The town hadn't officially begun its existence until 1884 when the Northern Pacific Railroad line to Winnipeg came through, but for the next forty-two years the carloads of wheat, potatoes, and barley attested to the wisdom of the location. Such a town would naturally attract businessmen.

It was in this relatively peaceful atmosphere on one Saturday night in early August that the people of Vingelen were startled to read that there would be a series of films at the new movie house. The posters, in rather smudgy black ink, showed a drawing of a Negro baby with the proclamation:

"Latest Movies from Hollywood!
Friday Night, August 27.
Free! Eleven-Month-Old Baby
to be Given Away!"

3

Out in the Field

3

It was over ninety degrees as Paul and Karl tossed the heavy bundles onto the rack. Karl, as usual, was thinking. Another threshing season! Another year of pitching somebody else's bundles into somebody else's machine, watching somebody else's barley come out and watching somebody else get the money. Oh well, I suppose there's some consolation in knowing that the prices are so low these days nobody can get rich. But where's it all going? Where am I going? Six years ago wheat was three bucks a bushel. I was gonna get a farm of my own--one with no cows--and make enough money so that I could go to the Agricultural College in the winters. That plan sure went sour!

Karl Thorson wanted to get a high school diploma and go to North Dakota Agricultural College, the A.C., in Fargo. So far, he had neither. His father had been forced to take a job in the Vingelen Elevator in the fall of 1920. The government had abruptly terminated the price supports that had placed the silver lining in the war clouds. Karl had been seventeen, old enough to take over farming and old enough to quit school. He had already gone to school three years longer than his parents had and besides, if Karl stayed home and farmed, his younger brother would be able to continue in school. It wasn't fair, of course, but everybody in the Vingelen area thought it quite natural. Karl was not expected to go into the ministry so a diploma wasn't necessary. Besides farming without an education was good enough for everybody else.

In fact, while education was generally considered to be a good thing, ambitions to be anything other than a farmer were looked upon with some measure of suspicion. Karl Thorson was a good farmer, but the mail sorter in the post office sent out the nasty and soon substantiated rumor that Karl was the only person in the Vingelen area ever to take correspondence school courses from Moorhead State Teacher's College. One more winter and he would have his high school diploma. Now, as he thought about his frustrated plans, he began to attack the load of bundles with a furious pace.

Simultaneously, the bundles flew and his thoughts raced. Plan A is to get some money, Plan B is to go to college. The result of Plan B would be to accomplish more of Plan A. All in all, it seems unlikely that by pitching this bundle into this stupid machine I am any closer to achieving Plan A. Three o'clock in the afternoon and I'm already sick of this. The most depressing thing about feeding the threshing machine is that I'm just an extension of it. The steam engine turns the wheel, the wheel turns the belt, the belt turns the thresher, the thresher turns me. What do I turn? Older!

What do you wanna do with your life, Karl? Nice question, Karl. Thank you for asking yourself that. Come to think of it, you're the only one who has ever asked that question. Everyone thinks they know. They think I'm gonna work for a few more years, marry a local Norwegian girl, live with Ma and Pa, have half a dozen yellow-haired kids, inherit the farm and, no doubt, inherit a debt, and buy a cemetery plot at the Småland Lutheran Church. Which part of this machine is going to wear out first? I got a feeling it's going to be me.

Proposition one! said Karl to himself as he pitched another bundle into the jaws of the threshing machine. Farmers are not dumb. Proposition two: (as another bundle flew), I am a farmer. Ergo, I am not dumb. Proposition three: Anybody who works everyday and gets nowhere is dumb. Proposition four: I work everyday and get nowhere. This is dumb! Proposition five: I am dumb. Proposition six: I am a farmer. Ergo, farmers are dumb. The last six bundles had been tossed into the machine, and he and Paul were ready to go out to the field to collect another load.

Paul stood next to Karl as they made their way back to the

field. With a venomous outburst Karl suddenly said, "And I suppose they want me to marry some local girl, keep my mouth shut, and keep putting money in everybody else's pocket."

Whatever Paul had expected Karl to say, it wasn't that. He asked Karl, "What in the hell are you talking about?"

"I mean, look at everyone in this threshing crew. Have they had an original thought all day? All week? In their lives?"

"What's that got to do with you getting married?" asked Paul in genuine bewilderment.

"I don't know, nothing I guess. It's just that I feel like it's time I got on with life. I like farming, I really do. But there's no reason one can't live a useful, creative and interesting life while doing so. Can you think of any girl around here who is creative and interesting?"

Paul began to leer, "What about..."

"*Ja*," Karl interrupted, knowing who Paul was about to suggest. "She certainly is interesting, but hardly creative."

"Oh, I dunno I hear she's done some pretty creative things with..."

"You know what I meant," said Karl with a withering expression of contempt, "I just want somebody who isn't entirely predictable and who won't be exactly like her Norwegian mother."

"What's the matter with that?" asked Paul indignantly. "Ma's a Norwegian mother."

"There you go then. Would you like to marry Ma?"

"I see what you mean," agreed Paul, "I suppose you wanna marry one of them Flappers, '23 Skiddo' and all that."

"*Ja*, maybe I wanna do just that," said Karl defensively.

"And bring her back to the farm? I can see it all now. You elope with Clara Bow. You bring her back to the farm, and you sit around quoting Theodore Dreiser."

"At least I want to marry somebody who has heard of Dreiser. What do you wanna bet you're the only other person on this crew who has read Dreiser? I mean, who has even heard of Dreiser?"

"*Ja*, I guess you're right."

"Of course I am. And that's the way it's going to be until some changes are made in this society."

Oh oh, thought Paul, now I've done it. Here comes the politics. He smiled inwardly so as not to upset his brother, and made himself comfortable leaning on the back of the wagon.

"And yet, the very people who would benefit from a change are the most resistant to it. Every darn time, Paul. Every darn time. Look at the last election. Who voted for Coolidge? The farmers! The Republicans were the single most devastating force against the farmer since the grasshopper, and who do the farmers vote for? Davis? A few did, even though I'll admit he wasn't a heck of a lot better than Coolidge. La Follette? The man who had been their champion for thirty years? Heck no, other than the good people of Wisconsin, of course. Eugene V. Debs? The only man with a program that could really make a difference? Hell, no! They voted for Coolidge. They would have voted for a grasshopper if they would have had the chance!"

"When they go ahead and vote for a political party which has every intention of fleecing them, they deserve to be fleeced. That's the drawback of a democracy when the majority of the people are idiots. I know, I know. That sounds like Mencken and I hate Mencken, but he is right sometimes. I hate to admit it, but he is." By this time Karl was gesturing to the horses as if they had disagreed with him.

"So what should they do, Karl?" said Paul, feeling that he had to jump into the argument for the sake of the unfortunate horses.

"Well, they could start by trying to gain back some of their own economic destiny..."

Paul had been hoping he would use that phrase. It was one of his favorites and it always indicated that Karl was going to launch into a declaratory sermon on the Non-Partisan League. In doing so, Karl would get worked up and pitch bundles at a furious pace, thus easing Paul's share. Karl stopped the wagon beside the first set of shocks but before tossing the first bundle, he continued his speech.

"If the League can own its own elevators, why not its own mills? Why not its own railroads? Look at the League in North Dakota. It was winning. It was going to make it. If they could have stuck together long enough to get complete control of the state they could have shown everybody. They nearly did, you know. And we got more farmers in Minnesota than they got out there!"

"Now, now Karl. Don't go siding with those Bolshies. You're likely to get put on the Red Ark and wake up in Russia."

"Bolshies! Bolshies?" Karl screamed.

Oh oh, thought Paul, I think I've gone a little far. He's even thrown down his fork in disgust.

"Listen, Paul, don't go badmouthing the Bolshies to me. I won't defend the way they sneaked out of the war or how they killed all those people, but at least they're trying something new. I say, give them a chance."

"All right, Karl, I will! And furthermore, I won't make you marry a local girl."

At that, Karl sheepishly bent down and picked up his fork and continued to pitch bundles. He looked up to see Paul grinning and pretty soon he was also grinning. They genuinely did like each other, and weren't afraid to let each other know it.

Karl and Paul both turned to their work, but before the wagon was half loaded Karl said, "*Uffda*, it's too hot to work this hard. Is there any water left in that jar?"

"*Ja*, but since you left it lying in the sun, are you sure you wouldn't rather have a cup of coffee?"

"You know, it might be ninety-five degrees out here, but a cup of coffee does sound good. How long till they bring out lunch?"

"Only about an hour! Why are we doing this kind of work, Karl?"

"Funny, I was asking myself the same question."

Karl and Paul were the younger sons of A.C. Thorson. The two sons knew, of course, what the A.C. stood for, but few other people in the Vingelen area had the slightest idea. A.C. had moved his family of four into the Red River Valley in 1905 and had left his father's homestead in southern Minnesota to his older brother. A.C. ran the threshing rig on days when he was not working in the Vingelen Co-op Elevator. This situation did not exactly please Karl and Paul who were quick to note that Pa did considerably less work than they did. However one allowed for the burdens of responsibility, it was undeniably harder work to pitch the forty-pound bundles high on the rack than it was to wander around the steam engine with an oil can.

"It isn't the heat, it's the *humility*," cracked Karl, and snickered at what, for him, had been an original pun. Paul nodded his head.

Paul wasn't particularly the silent type but this was one of those infrequent times when words were not forthcoming. Paul didn't like the heat any more than Karl. He wished he could think of more excuses for quitting, but as long as the other teams brought the bundles to the thresher, there didn't seem to be any alternative but to keep up. He looked up at the western sky with mixed emotions. If that high cloud on the horizon meant rain, he wouldn't have to haul bundles on Monday. On the other hand, if it rained, the barley would stain, the price would be lower, and after all, this was still a family farm. Besides, they weren't going to work tomorrow anyhow. Still, even that weak coffee that Mrs. Haugen made for the crew would taste good now.

"What the hell, Karl! This wagon's loaded high enough. Let's take her back," said Paul, as they came to the end of another row of shocks.

A strong south wind was blowing the chaff from the straw chute of the threshing machine as Karl and Paul got in line to unload their bundles. Karl was squinting into the wind but apparently not quite enough. A sharp pain in his left eye suddenly left him partially blind. His eye filled with tears and left him groping dangerously near the gaping jaws of the machine. Paul immediately knew what it was. Karl had made intimate contact with a barley beard. Scrambling quickly over to Karl's side of the rack, Paul led him down to the ground. Karl was cussing with a style and ingenuity seldom heard in civilian life. Paul tried to hold a cup of the warm, puce-colored drinking water to Karl's eye, but the barbs of a barley beard--like a hundred tiny fishhooks--held tightly to Karl's eye. There was nothing to be done but to take Karl to the doctor in Orebro.

It was an ill wind that blew no good. Paul not only could take the rest of the day off to take his brother to the doctor, but he had the satisfaction of knowing Pa would have to unload the whole rack by himself. Karl, still cussing in a mixture of Swedish, Norwegian, and English, was tenderly guided to the Haugen house and from there Paul took him home. Ma made coffee and while Karl was cleaning up for his trip to the doctor, Paul was able to eat his lunch in the house, away from the flies that always seemed to congregate around his jam and brown cheese sandwiches.

Moaning like it was his last day on earth and feeling as though it almost certainly was, Karl seemed to be in a hurry to get to the doctor. Therefore, with a fairly genuine concern, Paul went out to *put on* gas and get the Model T cranked up. In a short time they had begun their eight mile trip to Orebro. Paul enjoyed the ride. Karl swore every time they slowed down and, holding a damp rag to his eye, was sure that it had taken his grandfather less time to come from Sweden. As they reached town, Paul tried in vain to get Karl to at least cuss quietly as they passed the Orebro Parsonage.

Orebro was slightly larger than Vingelen, but otherwise it was essentially the same. It did have one hint of foreigners, however. On the south edge of town there was a Catholic church to serve the needs of some Southern Germans who had settled nearby. Although the visitors from Vingelen wondered what went on in *the fish house*, most were content to use their imagination rather than find out. Besides, those Catholics seemed to be all right otherwise. In fact, as Paul had learned in Vingelen the weekend before, they were having a wedding dance in the Orebro Community Building that night.

Parking the car in front of the doctor's office, Paul headed Karl up the steps and into the waiting room.

"Smells like a doctor's office," said Karl suspiciously.

"What did you expect?" asked Paul as they sat down on a hard bench in the doctor's waiting room.

"I don't know, but I don't like it. How long do you think I'll have to wait?" asked Karl nervously.

"I'll ask the nurse," said Paul and, with genuine compassion, asked Karl, "Would you like me to get you a magazine?"

"Get me a magazine? What would I do with that? I can't see with this rag in my eye. Tell him to hurry or I'll be blind the rest

27

of my life, " moaned Karl as he slumped farther down on the bench.

"It probably wouldn't hurt so much if you would just leave it alone," lectured Paul.

"*Fa'n i helvete!*" (Had this Norwegian phrase been translated into English, it would not have shocked a non-Scandinavian. To all moral and upright Scandinavians, however, the phrase was somehow much worse than its literal meaning, "Devil in hell!") You talk like I should ignore it. It hurts so much I could cry!"

"You are crying."

"Get me the doctor."

Politely Paul asked the nurse if the doctor could see his brother, explaining that it was somewhat of an emergency. The nurse methodically took down his name and, gesturing to the other four people in the waiting room, one of whom appeared to be holding part of a finger in one hand and a bloody bandage in the other, told him she would do her best. Paul went back and sat down with Karl.

"Did you know there's a dance in town tonight?" Paul tentatively suggested.

"How can I dance if can't see where I'm going?" roared Karl. "Besides, when we get done here we have to go back and haul more bundles."

"Well, I was coming to that. Ah, it seems as though there are a couple of emergency cases here before you. By the time the doctor gets that beard out, and by the time we get back home, it would be too late to thresh anymore. If the doc gets that out of your eye, we might just as well stay in town for a while."

"His brother is going blind, and he wants to dance," groaned Karl, although the pain didn't seem quite as bad as it had before he heard about the dance.

But, it is hard to think about a polka and a sore eye at the same time. At the moment, Karl was prone to think about his eye. The pregnant Norwegian woman, who sat beside him on the couch and could understand his Swedish cussing, moved to a chair in the corner of the room and superficially scanned a three-month old copy of the **Decorah Posten**. Paul was torn between sympathy for his brother and an unconcealed glee in seeing the woman blush. As the man with the cut finger was led into the doctor's office, Paul ventured to point out how calm he was compared to Karl. Karl growled an off-color suggestion about what he could do with that finger, and the lady with the crying child abruptly left the waiting room.

"If you keep that up, you'll be next," said Paul.

Karl did and, as it turned out, was next. Within five minutes the doctor had removed the barley beard. Karl was immensely relieved and uttered an embarrassed apology to the two women patients who had sought refuge in the hall. After a grim period of silence Karl added, "Uh, I guess you must be next, " and hastily followed Paul down the stairs.

Maybe they could have made it back to the Haugen farm to help for an hour or so, but Karl was feeling much better and they reasoned that it was foolish to ruin a good excuse just because it was no longer valid. They decided to stay for the dance.

The brothers had been to Orebro enough times to know a few girls or at least know who they were. During the winter the two consolidated schools would always play a home and away basket-ball series. Orebro usually won before the Schmidt brothers began playing basketball for Vingelen, but in the last three years, Vingelen had won almost every game it played and had participat-ed in the State Invitational Tourney in St Paul. The Thorson brothers usually went to these games by some means or other. In fact, Paul had even played basketball in high school although he hadn't been very successful. Karl wasn't very athletic, and besides, he had chores to do while the old man worked in the elevator.

It was during the high school basketball games, however, that the youth of the various communities had the best chance to meet one another. Mostly they hated each other if they had comparable teams, but looked kindly on those towns that were either perennial losers or perennial winners. Vingelen had been a perennial loser and was now an upstart as a winner. Even after high school, one still felt an obligation to hate the old rival, although one could be forgiving as far as girls were concerned. With Orebro, even this was hard but the boys were determined to try.

The thing that the followers of the Vingelen Vikings hated the most about the Orebro Dragons was that Orebro had to keep bringing up Knut Nelson. Knut had played for Vingelen almost six years ago. He was a tall, yellow-headed Swede whose face seemed to *hang out* and express a sincere nothing. It was not that Knut was not bright--in fact, his grades in school were above average. It was just that he did not look bright. Although born in America, he still hadn't learned much English and were it not for the fact that he liked basketball, he might have been content to do all of his learning at home. One night when Vingelen was scheduled to play a game in Orebro, Knut, his team's leading scorer, could not be located. He was finally found in the school building trying to find the dressing room saying "*Jeg har gått meg vill,*" (I'm lost). Those who knew Knut accepted this explanation as logical. Upon hearing about it, however, the Orebro crowd greeted Knut with a chant of "*Hvor er du*, Knut?" (Where are you?). Knut went on to play his most memorable game. Unfortunately, it was hardly his best. Orebro jumped into an early lead and it was obvious to all but Knut that it would be no contest. Eager to quiet the crowd, he was playing his heart out. Then late in the third quarter, as Knut was playing near the basket, a deflected pass seemed to float out of nowhere. He grabbed the ball and, to his amazement, there was no one in front of him. He started to lope down the floor in the direction of his own goal. Never a backcourt man, Knut streaked down the middle of the court dribbling the ball in high bounces that seemed to come just below his chin. However, as he reached his own free throw line, he appeared to trip over the paint and managed to spread his six-foot, two-inch frame over the basketball. The ball seemed to attach itself to his mid-section and acted as a ball bearing for one of sport's most memorable slides. He was not seriously hurt, but he did manage to break one of the boards that supported the basket post. The coach had immediately gone over to check on him, but was chuckling along with the rest of the crowd. The game was never finished. The referees provided the excuse by saying the basket was no longer centered, but everyone realized that the main reason was that members of both teams were laughing too hard. Knut didn't return to school until after Christmas.

Karl and Paul decided to have a hot beef sandwich at Carlson's Restaurant. With the exception of the lunches over at the hotel, it was the one place in Orebro to get a decent meal. The restaurant featured a high tin ceiling with large electric fans slowly blowing the strips of fly paper attached to the lights. Eleven stools covered in warm brown corduroy were bolted to the floor next to a counter covered with yellow linoleum. Perhaps it had once looked nice but cigarettes had burned a number of holes in the counter top, and over the years the holes had grown bigger as the patrons absentmindedly picked at the soft linoleum with their fingernails. Behind the counter was the menu printed on a blackboard with a bluish chalk. On the far wall five booths were occupied by five customers. There were two pool tables and a few nickel slot machines in the back room. It was clean enough, if you ignored the slimy cuspidor just inside the door.

Sig Carlson approached them from the kitchen, wiping his hands on his apron. No one minded Sig. In spite of a reputation as a sloth, inspired by his grossly overweight appearance, he actually worked quite hard in his restaurant. He made great hamburgers and thick malts, selling those he didn't consume. Occasionally, however, his brother Adolf would come into the restaurant to help him. Adolf was a livestock trucker and although he seemed to be careful about washing his hands, he could often be found in the kitchen with dried manure on his boots and cuffs. Although no one felt mean enough to call him such to his face, he was referred to as "Shitleg Carlson" for miles around. Luckily for Karl and Paul, Sig was in the restaurant alone tonight.

"You guys from Vingelen, ain't you?" asked Sig.

"*Ja*," mumbled Karl.

"*Hvor er* Knut? Ha, ha, ha, ha!"

"Lives down in Minneapolis now. Comes to see us every time we go down for the state tournament," answered Paul in a most superior manner.

"What'd ya want?"

"Hot beef sandwich and coffee."

"What'd ya want?"

"Hot beef sandwich and coffee."

As Sig ambled into the kitchen, Paul crowed; "Guess I told him, huh Karl?"

"Still going to cost us four bits apiece though," muttered Karl. "We gonna have enough to go to the dance?"

"Just barely," replied Paul.

"Any left over for a little visit to the bootlegger?" invited Karl.

"Not a chance," Paul ruefully admitted. "Besides, you can be sure Ma would find out about it if we did. She'll be waiting up to see how your eye is."

Karl mumbled agreement. The only safe place to sneak a drink was in Fargo where nobody knew them. The brothers sat in silence, sopping up the last of the rich brown gravy with their bread. Sig Carlson wandered over to refill their coffee cups.

"You're good to make coffee, know that Sig?" said Paul as his sleeve blotted the traces of gravy near his mouth.

"After the third refill, I charge a nickel a cup," replied Sig adroitly fielding the compliment.

After supper they walked down to the lake. It was still at least an hour before the dance would begin. Orebro had a nice park. Every year the Norwegians of the area gathered there on two occasions. *Syttende mai* (May 17th), the Norwegian Constitution Day, was probably the biggest day of the year. The *Hallings*, immigrants from the *Hallingdal* area of Norway, always challenged the *Trondheimers* in a tug of war, a rowing race, or some other manly sport. Immigrants from Østerdalen were also at the potluck picnic, but didn't enter into the intense rivalry that existed between the *Hallings* and the *Trondheimers*. Each group admitted to being Norwegian when among the Swedes, but when they were alone, they identified with their own parts of Norway. Although most were now one generation removed from the mountain valleys, each group maintained its own distinctive linguistic style and its own customs. Perhaps they didn't actually hate one another, but each group considered the other to be presumptuous and pushy. For their supposed willingness to get into knife fights, the former residents of *Hallingdal* were dubbed the *Kniv-Hallings*. Of course, none of them had ever used a knife in Orebro, but one just

32

knew how those people were.

The second major event of the year was the Fourth of July picnic. The activities were basically the same, but on the Fourth of July the language was English. The first generation of immigrants prided themselves on their knowledge of the history of their new land. On this day, at least, Abraham Lincoln was far more significant than St. Olaf. The Swedes of the Orebro and Vingelen areas generally avoided the *syttende mai* celebration. They felt a little bit like outsiders and, in a fit of Norwegian patriotism, an old Norwegian was sure to make some inflammatory remark about Sweden's possession of Norway from 1814 to 1905. The Swedes didn't have an identifiable substitute for *syttende mai*. While they were proud of being Swedish, they did not seem to possess the inbred love of the fatherland so common among Norwegians. The Swedes had adopted American customs and learned English earlier, and sometimes looked down on the Norwegians as their country cousins.

Between *syttende mai* and the Fourth of July, the Swedes held their Mid-Summer's Day picnic. This was always a church function usually held on the third Sunday of June at the church, or at the home of one of the larger farmers in the area. The church service was in Swedish, and the day was reserved for eating and sitting and sitting and eating. Not too many Norwegians attended this event. On the Fourth of July, however, the Norwegians and Swedes mixed.

It was this thought of mixing--socially, geographically, ethnically, and sexually--that occupied the current conversation of the Thorson brothers. It was cooler down by the lake, although the constant agitation of slapping mosquitoes tended to make one just as warm. Karl, without looking at his brother, said out of the corner of his mouth, "Do you think she'll be there tonight?"

Paul, perhaps truly ignorant of his brother's meaning, asked "Who?"

Karl wiggled his head in the general direction of the Orebro Park and said, "you know."

"You mean that girl that you met at Orebro's Fourth of July picnic?"

"*Ja.*"

"Was she from Orebro?"

"I don't know," admitted Karl. "I didn't get a chance to ask."

The vision of an unusual dark-haired girl gradually came back to Paul. He asked, "What was her name again?"

"I don't know that either. I only talked to her when you and Sven were trying to beat the Holmgren boys in that boat race. What'd you hafta row so darn fast for anyway?"

"Because Sven had gone ahead and bet a dollar, that's why," said Paul defensively. "Is she Swedish or Norwegian?"

"I don't know. She didn't sound either. We talked American all the time and she sounded sort of funny, like she didn't come from around here."

"You don't know much about her do you?" asked Paul.

"Enough to know I'd like to see her again," sighed Karl who with an air of hope and determination, began to turn in the direction of the dance hall. His eye had never felt better.

4

At the Dance

4

In the summertime, it stays light for a long time in northern Minnesota, and it was just starting to get dark as Karl and Paul made their way to the Orebro Community Building. It was a little bit larger than Vingelen's and quite a bit newer. In fact, the floor was hardly warped at all. Over in the brightest corner was the Scandinavian Polka Orchestra, a uniquely dressed ensemble consisting of a violinist, a drummer, and an accordion player. Nels Wahlstrom, the accordion player who worked in the bank during the daytime, wore his only black suit. He would rather have played the piano, but since there was none in the building and pianos did not travel well, his repertoire was limited to his accordion tunes. He also liked to sing, and while this was generally the low point of the orchestra's performance, (the time most men sneaked out for a short pull on the bottle), he never failed to stir the hearts of the crowd with his rendition of *Hils fra meg der hjemme.* Iver Johnson, no relation to the other thirty-four Johnson families in the Orebro region, played the drums in shirt-sleeves. He used to be a farmer and his father wanted him to be a farmer, but Iver had taken over the management of the Orebro Hotel and had made quite a success out of it. He was a good drummer, and was secretly practicing twirling the sticks and flipping them in the air. (It must be said of Iver, though, that he never did practice his drums when there were guests in the hotel.) Finally the maestro, the leader of the orchestra, was Big Bill Kjelland who was dressed in a bold plaid shirt. Big Bill, trained on the intricacies of the *Hardanger* fiddle with its extra resonating strings, probably could have gone on to greater things. He kept a picture of Ole Bull in his living room and could play *Seterjentens Søndag* better than anyone in the whole state. His greatest regret was that his parents had never been able to send him to study music at St. Olaf College, or at least at Concordia, Augsburg, Luther, or some other Norwegian-Lutheran college. But here he was, western Minnesota's finest auctioneer, spending his days bellowing bids or cajoling timid bidders, and his nights displaying his talents before semi-appreciative people. He would play *Nikolina* seven times a night and cringe when the inevitable *en gang til* (one more time) escaped the throat of some drunken yahoo. Still, the music had its own rewards, and Big Bill was not above slipping in a classical piece by Grieg when no one seemed to be dancing anyhow. All in all, it was a remarkably talented orchestra, players who loved their work and were appreciated by all listeners. Remarkable too, was the fact that here was a three-piece band of Scandinavian-Lutherans playing for a Catholic wedding dance. That never would have happened in the old country.

Julie Morrison had no appreciation for the old country. She didn't have one. There was no Scandinavian lineage on either side of her family and she was glad. At times, though, she felt a little bit envious of people who seemed to belong to someone or somewhere. She could trace the Morrison line all the way back to her grandfather, whom she had never met, but who, according to her father had "come from Kentucky, I think." Her mother's maiden name had been Smith and in answering a curious musing of Julie's, her grandmother had told her, "Well, it's English, I guess, but there's some Scottish and Irish too, and somebody once said there was Pennsylvania Dutch in there someplace. That's why I got those little windmill curtains that hang in the kitchen." Julie, who had just finished reading about immigration in school, knew that the Dutch were really the "Deutsch." In the aftermath of World War I, however, she and many other Americans had decided to ignore ethnic ties altogether. Now here she was, holding the arm of some German at a Catholic dance in the middle of New Scandinavia.

Julie, as usual, was thinking. What am I doing here? Why am

I hanging on to this farmer? His hands look like he washed them in pure lye and they still smell of the barn. I should have stayed back in the hotel and read. No, I couldn't have done that again. I just wish that I could feel like I belong somewhere. At least these farmers have a home. What do I have? A hotel room. They have parents and chores and cows and horses and chickens and pigs and other things that breathe, care for them, or at least depend on them. What do I have? I've got Father.

Julie never wanted to stand out in a crowd. She always tried to find the back row or the least conspicuous part of the room. Yet, in a room full of blonde farm girls she stood out like a white crow. Her dark brown hair had absolutely no curl in it and, what there was of it, hung straight down. In contrast to the other girls of the area who often found it necessary to work outside, Julie's skin had little tan and the darkness of her hair made her skin look unnaturally white. This tended to make her green eyes all the more striking. Furthermore, it was 1926, and even though many of the local girls had not discovered rouge and lipstick, Julie knew how to use them and use them well. As she looked at the line of other young men waiting to dance with her, her self-pity increased.

I'm the only woman here with a store-bought dress. I hate it. I hate it not only because it's a cheap thing with poor material and shoddy construction, but because every other woman here hates me for having it. I wish I could sew. I wish I lived in a real house where I could have a mother who could teach me to sew. These other women do not realize that I envy them and their homemade clothes. It's almost enough to make me willing to marry a farmer. Almost, but not quite. I've not met a man who could make me want to live in the country and smell cows.

But, I wish I belonged somewhere. Until last year I could name almost all the towns in Minnesota and North Dakota where we had lived. Now I don't even remember the number. Still, in a way, going from small town to small town isn't too bad, at least they're mostly the same and it is probably better than living in the city. Here we can be poor and not be any worse off than anyone else.

I'll never forget how I hated that senior year in Minneapolis. I wish I could have graduated from a small town high school like Orebro. All these people share something of which I will never be a part. If they knew how lucky they were, they wouldn't envy my store-bought dress and, if I didn't have to wear it, they might be a little friendlier. Hmm, where have I seen that guy before?

Karl's eye was definitely better. He was using it now to scan chairs around the sides of the hall in search of the girl he had been thinking of ever since they had met. The music ended and, sure enough, there she was. She was tenderly holding the arm of some German. Karl wasn't sure how he knew he was a German, but he did. Somehow that realization pleased him because he figured it wouldn't be difficult to take her away from him. Before the next tune began, he sauntered up and asked her to dance.

Karl had never considered that she may refuse him, and she didn't. In fact, she seemed as delighted to see him as he was to see her. As the Scandinavian Polka Orchestra struck up a new tune, she slipped her arm into his and let him lead her to the floor.

Karl thought his voice was unnaturally loud as he said: "I was hoping I would see you tonight. I never did get to ask you your name and, I wasn't even sure you were from Orebro."

She looked at him and smiled. "I was pretty sure you weren't from here. Who are you, anyway?"

"I suppose it's time that I introduce myself," Karl said in his most exaggerated manner. "My name is Karl Thorson."

"Very nice to meet you, I'm sure," she said with a giggle. (Cute laugh, thought Karl.) "My name is Juliette Morrison, but my friends call me Julie."

"Then I hope that I may call you Julie," said the gallant Karl. "I suppose you get tired of Romeo jokes, huh?"

"You don't know the half of it. My father, who gave me the name, is the worst of all. Every time he sees me talking to a man he asks, "Who's the Romeo? Then he roars as if he has said it for the first time."

"Is your father some kind of Shakespeare scholar?" asked Karl, wondering if he would be called Romeo before the night was over.

Questions about her father always embarrassed Julie. She

concentrated on her moving feet and replied, "Actually, no. He's ah, well, it's a little hard to tell you what my father does. He's sort of a salesman. I don't think he has read any Shakespeare other than Romeo and Juliet. In fact, I'm not even sure he has read that. He just wants people to think he is well educated because it helps in sales."

"What does your father sell?" asked Karl, his curiosity growing considerably.

"At the moment, I'm not sure that he sells anything. He's sort of between jobs. He was talking yesterday about picture shows. Before that, he sold patent medicines."

The edge of Karl's mouth started to twitch. The name Morrison was not uncommon, but how many Morrison's sold medicine? Oh God, he thought, could this be Doc Morrison's daughter?

"We only returned to this part of the country shortly before I talked to you at the picnic," Julie continued. "We had been living down in the cities the past two years. To tell you the truth, I wasn't really very happy about coming back here."

Karl's mind was racing. Two years ago! It's got to be his daughter!

"But where are you from, Karl?" she was suddenly asking.

Karl realized that this was no time to lie; it was just time to act innocent. "Oh, I'm from a little town about ten miles away. You've probably never heard of it."

"I don't know. I've probably been there. I did quite a bit of traveling with my father when we were here last time. What's it called?"

Karl tried to say the word naturally, but it came out in sort of a whisper. "Vingelen."

"What did you say?"

This time it seemed to Karl as though he shouted it. "Vingelen!"

Julie abruptly stopped dancing. "I hate that town and everybody in it," she said calmly as though it were a religious tenet.

"Well, I don't actually live there," Karl hastened to add. "I live on a farm about four miles away, uh, almost as close as from there to Orebro. I mean, from here to my place is closer than, uh, well, just because I went to school there, uh, I mean, from my place to Orebro is almost as close as from my place to Vingelen. Uh, the music seems to have stopped."

The music had indeed stopped. Karl and Julie were the only ones on the dance floor. Paul stood along the wall motioning for Karl to get off the floor. Hurriedly, and a bit awkwardly, they did.

By the time Karl found a chair for Julie, she seemed to have forgiven him for being from Vingelen. "I'm sorry," she said, "I know that was unfair. It's just that I have such horrible memories of that town. Let me explain."

Karl braced himself.

"About two years ago, my father did a show in Vingelen. He even got a permit to do the show in the community building. Things had been a little rough for us at the time; we didn't have a car, and we had to travel from town to town in a horse-drawn wagon. I didn't mind. In fact I really loved the horse. But anyway, when we got to Vingelen, Dad made camp on a hill overlooking the lake. It really was a pretty spot to camp, and I had high hopes for our stay there. I went into town with Dad to help him set up. We came back to our camp and had supper and when he went into town to do the show, I stayed behind to look after the horse and wagon.

"Well, Dad said the show went all right until near the end, just when he was about to make his sales pitch for 'Doctor Morrison's Electrical Elixir.' It seems that some guys had seen the show before in another town and they came to Vingelen just to foil one of Dad's magic acts. One of them yelled that he had bought a bottle of Electrical Elixir and had gotten drunk even though he never drank because drink was the tool of the devil, and he wanted everyone to know that Electrical Elixir was as bad as whiskey. That in itself would have been funny, because there was nothing in it that could have made anyone drunk. I helped Dad make it up myself. It was only water and molasses and some spices and some powders that were good for headaches. Anyway, it seemed that the claim that it made a person drunk would help sales more than hurt them. Then someone else tried to defend Dad by pointing out that the Electrical Elixir was nothing more than water and molasses. At this point someone jumped up and asked him if he were the same Doctor Morrison who had been arrested for fraud in Fargo. Now, Father is a semi-honest man and resented the charge enough to ask the man to step outside. He didn't, but other people wanted to and after all that, well, Dad said he just needed a little drink."

"Gee, I'm sorry," offered Karl, "those things usually don't happen in Vingelen."

"Wait! For that I could forgive a town. Worse things than that have happened in many towns. It just sort of goes with the job. But, while Dad was off trying to find the bootlegger, some of your townsfolk came to our camp. By this time, I was sound asleep in the wagon. All of a sudden I was awakened by a few bumps and one giant splash. Water covered the floor of the wagon and ruined all my clothes. Dad finally came home, stewed to the gills, to find all our worldly possessions in the lake and me crying in front of a fire that had gone out a long time ago. I never want to see your town again and I hope you don't blame me."

"Of course not," said Karl grandly. "I just hope to prove to you that not all of the Vingelen people are like that. May I have this dance?"

As Karl traipsed across the floor he thought of two things. First, he had to get to Paul to tell him to keep his mouth shut. Second, he was trying to defend himself. "It was just a good prank," he thought. "We never would have pushed it in if we had known there was someone in there."

Karl totally forgot what dance he was supposed to be doing, but fortunately, his feet didn't. He finished the dance with what he considered to be a certain degree of aplomb. As Karl and Julie walked back to the edge of the hall, Paul came up to them with a grin that combined envy and appreciation. Karl immediately took the offensive in what could have become a ticklish situation.

"Uh, Paul, uh, I'd like you to meet Julie Morrison," to which Karl quickly added in a frantic whisper, "Ixnay on the agonway. Julie, I'd like you to meet my brother, Paul."

"Very nice to meet you, Julie," said Paul. "What's this about a wagon?"

"I beg your pardon?" said Julie innocently.

"Karl quickly stepped in between them adding, "Julie MOR-RIS-ON has traveled around this country in a wagon."

Paul's face looked blank. Then he blinked. Then he smirked. The message had been understood. "Perhaps we should be traveling too, Karl. Unless you're willing to stick another barley beard in your eye, we got chores to do tomorrow."

"*Ja*, I suppose it's time to go. Go out and start the car. I'll be with you in a few minutes."

As Paul walked out, Karl was eager to change the subject to something he had been thinking about ever since he saw her. When could he see her again? "I'd like to see you again. Will you be staying in Orebro long this time?" Karl heard himself ask.

"I'm not really sure. My father is trying to arrange something so I'm not sure where we will be. We are staying in the hotel here in the meantime."

"Are you there with your mother most of the time?" asked Karl hopefully.

"My mother died when I was nine. That's mostly why I travel with my father. He really is a dear man, but he does need someone to take care of him."

"Well then, perhaps I will stop at the hotel sometime and see you."

As Karl blushed, Julie smiled and said, "That would be nice."

Karl said good night and practically ran from the hall. Paul was waiting in the car and started driving as soon as Karl's foot hit the running board.

"Pa's going to be mad as hell. We gotta make sure we have our story straight. You don't think he would really ask the doctor what time he got done with you, do you?" asked Paul.

"Nah. Besides, I think he would have done the same thing. He ain't such a bad guy. And the way those Iverson boys were pitching bundles, nobody probably even missed us. Let's just not mention the dance unless we are asked."

The young men drove on in silence for a time. Then, Paul started to giggle. "So that was Doc Morrison's daughter, eh? Did her old man tell her about how his wagon got shoved in the lake?"

"He didn't have to. She was in it."

"When we pushed it in the lake? No."

"Yup."

"I presume you didn't brag about the fact that you were the pusher and she was the pushee."

"Nope."

"Gonna see her again?"

"Yup."

"Gonna tell her how you pushed her in the lake?"

"Nope."

5

Saturday Night
in Town

5

It was Saturday night again. Time to go to town. Karl was hoping to go to Orebro, but there was still threshing to do at the Halverson farm. Mrs. Halverson served the best threshing dinner in the Red River Valley, but her husband managed to balance this pleasure with being the hardest driving farmer of any they threshed for. To be sure, he led by example, loading bundles at a furious pace. Everyone was certain it would lead to a heart attack, and it did--the very next year. On this Saturday, Milo Halverson was working harder than ever. He was certain that it would rain all day Sunday and he wanted his wheat in. If this meant threshing until dark, they would thresh until dark. As it turned out, they did, and it rained all day Sunday.

By the time Karl finished threshing on Saturday night, did chores, washed up, ate supper, and shaved, it was already almost 9:00. Going to Orebro was out of the question, but there was still time to go to Vingelen to swap lies and dirty stories.

Unfortunately, Pa also wanted to go to town. If Karl wanted to borrow the car, he had to take the owner along. After some discussion, Ma decided she wanted to go along too. Pa was 46, exactly twice as old as Karl. Ma was 44, exactly twice as old as Paul. Karl had made the discovery of this amazing arithmetic ratio one day at the dinner table. Pointing out how the ratio would change at the next birthday, never again to be repeated, he had been met with unanimous disinterest. That disappointed Karl. He thought it was just the kind of fact that would fascinate Pa.

Some people maintained that Karl's streak of independence

was inherited from A.C. and, in truth, many of his political leanings had rubbed off on Karl. Pa had already lost much of the dark brown hair that had concealed a curiously lumpy skull. Now he kept what he had in sort of a wispy pompadour which was plastered down only when he went to town.

Pa had been born in America. His father came from Sweden as a young man and arrived just in time to serve in the Civil War. He had been a hero of sorts and when he died at a ripe old age, his body laid in state in the rotunda of the Minnesota State Capitol. Pa was in his late thirties when America joined the Great War. He was too old to serve in the war and his sons were too young. Privately, Pa was glad that he didn't have to go to France. Shooting at people disgusted him almost as much as getting shot at scared him. Publicly, however, he behaved like a great second generation patriot. After all, many of the people in the Vingelen region, including Ma, hadn't even been born in this country.

Ma's parents had sailed from a rocky island in the middle of a Norwegian *fjord*. For generations the Bjerke family had tried to eke out an agricultural existence on that island raising a few cows and goats and too many children. Finally, her parents took their six children and came to Minnesota. She was only six at the time, but she remembered how everybody was seasick. She still refused to get in a boat at Detroit Lakes. If one were to describe Ma, the word "medium" would be used frequently. She was of medium height, medium weight, and of medium intelligence. She had medium blue eyes and medium blonde hair. She was attractive, but not stunning. This combination produced a being that virtually nobody could dislike. Ma's folks were disappointed when she married a Swede, but that was twenty-five years ago so Ma and Pa were living proof that Vingelen's version of a "mixed marriage" could work.

Both Ma and Pa had put on their town clothes. There was little difference between Ma's town clothes and her church clothes, except that her town dress was usually a few years older than her church dress. Pa wore his church shoes, his church pants, and his church hat but left his tie and church coat at home. He somehow managed to roll his sleeves up higher than the sleeves on his work shirt, so an inch of almost dazzling white skin appeared in a narrow strip between his blue shirt and his deep tan skin. All in all, a nice couple. People looked forward to talking to Ma and Pa in the cafe be it about crops, the weather, or politics.

Paul had been planning to stay home but as Karl started to leave the yard, Paul jumped on the running board.

"So you're coming along, tew?" said Pa. "I tought yew vere tew tuckered out. So now ve got da whole Torson famley along, then."

Paul could think of no reasonable argument to that statement and kept still for a change. The sun had just set and there wasn't a breath of wind. As they drove past Refsal Slough, the herons seemed totally unconcerned and the ducks floated so idly that they seemed to be painted on glass. Karl appreciated such common beauty, but he did not feel the necessity of starting a conversation. He knew his Pa and Ma loved those kind of scenes as much as he did because they had, after all, taught him to notice and enjoy them. At one point Ma actually said, "Ah," and the rest of the family merely nodded in acknowledgement.

When they got to Vingelen, Ma had only about fifteen minutes before Nelson's Store closed. Karl and Paul dropped Ma and Pa off at the store and headed for the social focus of the village, the Castle Garden Inn.

Before the advent of Ellis Island, Castle Garden had been the chief entry terminal in New York for European immigrants. Most of the Scandinavian immigrants in the Vingelen area had come to America before Ellis Island had opened. The name of the inn still had nostalgia for a few of the residents of the Vingelen area but most thought it curious, if not ridiculous. Outside the cafe several men--middle-aged to elderly--sat occasionally spitting, scratching, and/or smoking. Inside the cafe the women sat and visited in the booths along the walls. Shopping was completed and groceries were in their cars. No woman here ever smoked, of course, but they did drink coffee and eat cookies and doughnuts. Down the middle of the cafe ran three sets of railroad car seats. These were near the pool tables and became the province of the teenagers and young adults. On one wall at the opposite side of the room from the booths was a high bar where some of the older men sat on stools remembering how they used to drink beer. There had been no ordinance about it, but this was the only place in the cafe where beer had been served and consumed. There was room for only six stools at the high bar and where that ended, a lower coffee counter began. This counter, with nine low stools, continued toward the kitchen which consisted of an ice-box, an oven, a large sink, and a large and amazingly greasy grill. Delmonico's it was not, but everyone considered the inn their own social center and a prime community asset.

There was another cafe in town, somewhat smaller. It had a larger beer bar and more cards were played there. Fewer women went in this cafe. It was said that it was easier to make contact with a bootlegger there, but no one could ever prove that. It served a definite need, if for no other reason than to handle the overflow from the Castle Garden Inn. It was called Flora's even though its real name was the East End Cafe. Flora presided over it with a matronly air that kept card-cheating and cussing at a minimum.

Karl parked the car in front of Flora's. It bothered him to do so since he was intending to walk by and go up to the Castle Garden. Flora was a good old soul and he thought he should patronize her cafe once in a while, but he seldom did.

As they walked into the cafe, they noticed a group of young men huddled around a sign on the back wall. In the space between the two wall racks for the pool cues, someone had put up a sign advertising *Latest Movies from Hollywood*.

"Hey, they're finally going to use that movie hall," said Paul. "We're going to get the latest movies from Hollywood. I suppose that means that we'll finally get those wonderful patriotic war movies from 1917 that we've heard so much about."

The more optimistic Karl responded, "Give 'em a chance. Maybe we'll get a Fairbanks or a Valentino picture. Sure would beat having to go all the way to Detroit Lakes just to see a movie, wouldn't it?"

"*Ja*, I suppose it would. What's that baby stuff?"

"It says here that an eleven-month-old baby will be given

away," said Karl, in a tone combining indignation and curiosity.

Paul took off his glasses, cleaned them, and examined the poster.

"A baby person? A human baby?" said Paul.

"I donno. They got a picture of a baby human there, don't they?" reasoned Karl.

"But they can't do that. They can't do that, can they?"

"I don't know. What would you do with a baby if you won one, Paul?" said Karl, gently shoving his brother towards a table.

"I haven't any idea, that's why I don't plan on entering the drawing. Uh, still... I suppose that I could give it away... Or maybe even sell it. Do you have any idea how much a baby is worth?"

"It could be, you know, that you won't win," Karl warned.

"Hey," Karl called across to a group of young men now sitting in the railroad seats. "Any of you guys know what this is all about?"

"Just what it says, I suppose," said Knut Andersson, a tall, gangly, blonde Swede. "In a few weeks we're gonna have the pictures and someone is going to give away a baby. Any of you guys been up to something you ain't bragging about?"

Sigurd Nelson, a broad muscular Norwegian, sniggered, "I wouldn't talk, Knut, after the way you've been carrying on with that Hanson girl. Come to think of it, we ain't seen her for a long time."

"Well, I seen her last week," protested Knut Andersson's brother Clarence, "and I can promise you it isn't something to do with her and Knut. Heh, heh, she won't even go out with him anymore, will she Knut?"

"Shut up, Clare. You didn't do any better with Maren Peterson, did you?" At this everybody except Clarence Andersson laughed.

The Andersson brothers, the Thorson brothers, Sigurd Nelson, Charles Holm, and Reidar Simonsen were crowded around the old railroad seats constituting about half the usual group that gathered on Saturday nights. They would swap lies, jokes and dirty stories; drink Coke or coffee; and share some dreams. For the most part they were ambitious young men if ambitious meant possessing the capacity to work hard to achieve a goal. Furthermore, their ambitions did not constitute outlandish dreams. Both the Andersson brothers wanted to become farmers. So did Sigurd Nelson and Charles Holm. Reidar Simonsen already had a job with the railroad, but he talked as though he would get into farming if he had the chance. Since he was the third oldest brother and his two older brothers were already farming with "the old man", there didn't seem to be much hope of it. The Thorson brothers were different. Their old man farmed, of course, but since he also managed the grain elevator much of the farm work was left to Karl and Paul. Although Pa was still a long way from retirement, no one ever came right out and said so. Everyone knew that one day Karl or Paul would run the farm. Paul made no secret of the fact that he didn't want to farm for the rest of his life. He loved motors, be they tractor or auto, and he wanted to become a mechanic and live in a city like Fargo.

Sometimes Karl wondered if he really wanted to become a farmer. He read a lot. He read novels--a curious blend of dime novel trash and the world's great literature--but he also read science, books on horticulture, and most of all, history. Farming was a good life, no doubt about that, but he really wanted to be an historian. He knew that his father--even if he had an extra dime, which he didn't--wouldn't give it to him to go to college to study history. Being a historian was out of the question. But what about a farmer-historian or a historian-farmer? After all, farming offered the kind of life he really wanted. Sure, the days were long in the summer and there were always chores to do, but in the winter-- once the cows were milked and the barn was cleaned--there was time to read. Let the snow pile up, as long as he could get to the Moorhead Library once in a while. Give me a good book, a pot of coffee, and a warm house. What else is there? Oh yeah, a good woman. I wonder if I'll ever see that Julie Morrison again? Maybe, if we are done with threshing by then, I could borrow the car and drive to Orebro, pick her up and take her to the movies. I could tell her she would have a chance to win a baby. I bet that would go over big.

"Isn't it, Karl?"

"Huh?" said Karl.

"Jeez, what are you dreaming about?" asked Charlie. "I was just asking you if it wasn't better to just burn straw off the field and be done with it. Paul was giving me some bullshit about plowing it under because it made the soil better. You ever get that straw stuck in the plow? Martha Goose! It took me an hour once just to clean it out. You set that stuff on fire and you can plow it an hour later and it goes through the plow like shit through a goose."

Karl now realized that he had not heard what anyone had said for the last several minutes. "'Fraid Paul's right, Charlie. Not only does the straw return nutrients to the soil, but it also enables the soil to have a higher humus content so it will retain moisture better. I suppose you might want to burn off the straw in an area where the grain was badly lodged, but you shouldn't do it unless you have to," Karl responded.

"I suppose you got that out of your books too, didn't you, Karl?" said Charlie, in a mixture of admiration and disgust.

"Well no, it's what Pa always says, but I have read about it in books, too," said Karl, eager to defend himself against the charge that he was actively pursing education.

After a somewhat embarrassing pause, Reidar interjected, "Did you hear about when *Lena* went to the doctor?" Most probably had, but that never stopped the blond Norwegian, whom Paul had once unkindly described as being "so short that every time he farts, he blows sand in his shoes." The Norwegians had a marvelous sense of humor when it came to telling jokes on themselves, but a somewhat less than marvelous sense of humor when others told jokes about them. Somehow, the characters were always *Ole* and *Lena*, and the jokes were always told with an exaggerated Norwegian brogue. A visitor from the East would have been hard pressed to tell the difference between an exaggerated brogue and Reidar's regular speech, but then a visitor from the East was also rare.

"*Lena* went to the doctor, see?" began Reidar, "and he asked her what was the matter. She says, 'Nottin' da matter wit me, it's *Ole*. He has trouble wit his bottom.' So the doctor, he says, 'What do you mean, Mrs. Olson? He has trouble with his bottom?' So *Lena* says, 'I mean, you know, he goes to da outhouse, but nottin' come out,' and the doctor says, 'You mean he's constipated, Mrs. Olson?' Well, *Lena* agrees that must be it, alright. The doctor gives her a little jar of suppositories and tells her that *Ole* should take them and he will be all right in a day or so. Well, a week goes by and then the doctor sees *Lena* in the street and he asks her how *Ole* is and she says that he is worse than ever. 'Well,' the doctor says, 'How can that be? Didn't he take those suppositories I sent with you?' And *Lena* tells him, '*Ja*, but for all da good it done him, he could'a yust as well shoved 'em up his ass.'"

The guys laughed like they had never heard it before and everyone else in the cafe looked up and knew right away that Reidar had told another dirty joke. The women shook their heads and the men made a mental note to find out what that was all about. Reidar, encouraged by the reception, continued.

"Well then, did I tell you about when *Ole* and *Lena* went on their honeymoon to Duluth?"

Karl sat there smiling with the rest of the young men, but he really wasn't listening. A live baby, he thought, how could they do that? Maybe Pa would let me use the car to pick up Julie and take her to Vingelen. Now I gotta think of an excuse to go back to Orebro to ask her. I don't much want to go back to the doctor again. I really should go to a dentist, but since the only dentist around here is in Ulven I don't suppose that does me any good. Maybe I can break something that can only get fixed in Orebro. Nah, I don't want to do that. I suppose I could write her a letter, but then she might write one to me and I don't want that sent to the farm and have to explain that to Ma. I know I'm twenty-three years old and I don't have to explain things to Ma, but still, ... I don't know.

There I go again, thinking like a thirteen-year-old. My life's half over and here I am living with the folks--no car, no property, no prospects, and no adventure. Buffalo Bill rode the Pony Express as a boy. When Billy the Kid was my age he had been dead for two years. Hmmm, I guess that's an argument against adventure. Nevertheless, there are guys my age who own businesses and serve on the school board. When Pa was my age, he already had a kid and was independent of Grandpa. And Grandpa Bjerke wasn't a heck of a lot older than I am when he left Norway.

If I just had the nerve to go up to Pa and say I wanna use the car to go courtin' this girl in Orebro, he would be happy to let me or at least he wouldn't mind too much. Of course, I'd have to put up with all of the "... 'ain't none of da girls around here good enough for yew den?" stuff. And if Ma heard, which Pa would see to in short order, I'd have to put up with, "Who is she? What does her father do?" and of course, "She's Lutheran, isn't she?" For all I know, she could be Catholic or even Jewish. Boy, would that go over like a turd in a punch bowl.

Nah, as usual I suppose I'll just waste my time on some dumb plan that will never pan out, and I'll procrastinate and fool around and by the time I get around to it, she will be gone and I'll end up marrying some dull local girl who...

"So, he got up and bought a ticket to Superior," finished Reidar. Everyone roared, including Karl who hadn't heard the rest of the joke.

6

Chores: Time
to Ponder

6

Karl loved Sunday mornings. The old man let everybody sleep late. It was already six-thirty and Karl was just starting the milking. The Halverson boys had been in the barn since five o'clock. Pa had a much better attitude than Mr. Halverson. Every other day in the summer, Pa said chores had to be started by five although old man Halverson kept telling Pa how important it was that the cows be milked everyday at exactly the same time in exactly the same order. Pa was never swayed by that argument, and for that Karl was grateful. Anyway, church didn't start until nine o'clock so that left them with plenty time to finish the chores and have a second cup of coffee before going to church.

The Thorson family, like everyone else in the area, didn't think much about going to church. They just went. It was like chores in the morning. You just did it. Lately there had been a drop-off in attendance for the Swedish language services, but that was expected and accepted. If you only spoke American, then it probably wouldn't do you much good to go. Still, it was a time to get together to see who didn't go, and then wonder why they weren't there. The Sunday following an absence would always bring the inevitable, "Where were you last Sunday, then?" or perhaps, "Were you out on a toot last weekend?" For the sake of appearances, the grilled absentee usually had a solid excuse.

As far as chores went, Karl didn't mind doing them. He accepted them as part of life. Paul didn't feel that way and could never see the correlation between the sun coming up and doing the chores. Occasionally the brothers would take turns doing each other's chores, and although Paul was by now several turns behind Karl, that fact didn't really bother either of them. Today was one such day. Paul had claimed that he just couldn't face a four-legged animal so, for a time at least, the barn belonged to Karl, six milk cows, the dog, and eight cats. Before long, Ma would be along to do the milking. Karl, of course, had done his share of milking but as far back as he could remember, it was always Ma who was the chief milker in the family. This followed tradition as much as inclination. All the farm women in the Vingelen area did the milking and looked after the chickens just as their mothers had done back in the old country. Karl had heard, many more times than he wanted to, stories about how tough it had been for Grandma back in Norway. As a young girl she had been a milkmaid, a *jente*, and spent her summers high up in the mountains in a cabin called a *sæter* while the cows, undazzled by the rugged beauty, grazed on summer grass. At the *sæter* she milked the cows twice a day and stored the milk in small vats where it soured to just the right consistency. When she was not milking, she carried baskets of manure on her head up the side of the mountain to fertilize the small fields that probably shouldn't have been cultivated in the first place. Ma felt that these days, on this fertile and level prairie, the people had it "too easy."

Some of Karl's earliest memories were of Ma sitting alongside a guernsey cow on a wobbly milk stool. Ma usually kept her head, which was always wrapped in a scarf, resting on the smooth flank of the cow. When Karl and Paul had been children, they sat a short distance away and Ma would tell them fairy tales while she milked. As long as Karl lived, he would never forget about "**Little Peter Pastureman**" or "**When Mother Troll Took in the King's Washing**." He wondered if he would ever get married, and if his wife would milk cows and tell his children about trolls and *tomter*. Such thoughts naturally led to Julie.

Not that Karl was ready to think about marrying Julie, but he was certainly ready to think about seeing her again. The more he thought about it, the more certain he was that he should take her to Vingelen to see the movies. Ma came in, and soon Karl could hear the rhythmic squirts of milk into the bottom of the shiny new milk pail that Ma had bought the night before.

"Well Ma, does it work?" Karl inquired.

"*Ja*, it sure seems to. Now if only I can get Blossom to fill it like she did the last one. I think she's drying up at last."

This was typical of the extent of their conversations the last few years, but now Karl asked, "Remember the story about *Smørbal*?"

Ma suddenly stopped milking, rocked back on her milk stool, and smiling wistfully said, "Oh, I don't think so. I haven't told those stories for years. Why? What made you think about that?" asked Ma.

"I donno," fibbed Karl. "I guess I saw those horse shears and thought about *Smørbal's* little scissors."

"*Ja*, that *Smørbal* was a smart one," recollected Ma, and returned her attention to Blossom.

Ma soon had the first cow milked and Karl got busy cranking the handle on the cream separator. The cream would be stored in the tall steel cans and kept in the cooler until it was brought to the creamery Wednesday night. The cooler was a little building next to the windmill. When the cold water came up from the ground, it was piped through a cooling tank before it ran into another pipe leading to the stock tank. It was generally adequate as a refrigerator. As the cream ran from the separator into a small can, the skimmed milk went into a large pail. This was what the eight cats had been waiting for ever since Karl came into the barn. He picked up the can and walked over to the filthy cat pan. Kicking cats out of the way in a gentle but firm manner, he emptied the pan of its accumulated straw and insects and poured the skimmed milk into it. The cats greedily crowded around and drank their fill. At this, Karl always had two thoughts: Why do we have so many cats? And, Why do I give them so much milk that they aren't hungry enough to go mousing?

As he was working, he kept thinking about going to Orebro again to see Julie. Every Wednesday night for as long as he could remember the family had gone into Vingelen to bring the cream to the creamery and the eggs to the hatchery. They had never gone to Orebro.

"Ma, how come we never take the eggs and cream to Orebro? I hear they pay a real good price for 'em there." Actually, Karl had no idea what they paid for eggs or cream in Orebro, but he reasoned it couldn't be too much less than it was in Vingelen.

"Because we have always brought the cream to John Knutson's," said Ma, as if that totally explained the situation. "I suppose it doesn't make much difference one way or the other though, since we don't get much for them anyway. Why do you ask?"

"Well," Karl hesitated, "you know when me and Paul went to Orebro a while ago, when Paul took me to the doctor? I just noticed that it looked like a pretty nice creamery. They built it a couple years ago. I thought maybe we ought to give it a try once. It ain't much further to Orebro than to Vingelen, and the road is just as good."

"I guess I don't care that much about John Knutson one way or the other," admitted Ma, as she crossly knitted her eyebrows. "We didn't even get a decent calendar from him last Christmas. He used to be so good to give Christmas presents, but in the last couple a years it's been darned slim pickings from him. I do like to go into the restaurant in Vingelen though."

Karl smiled to himself. He knew that the week after next Ma was having Missionary Prayer Circle at her house. Missionary Prayer Circle was more than an organization for the women of the church. It was the one day of the year that his mother looked forward to with both fear and anticipation. There were three circles in the congregation. Ma belonged to the Naomi Circle. Once a month, all year long, circles would meet at the home of one of the members. The number of people at circle was usually about twice the membership, for each woman often brought a guest. As the guest was usually a member of one of the other two circles, a healthy percentage of the female population of the church was always present. At circle, someone was always in charge of Bible study and devotions, and another person was in charge of special entertainment. Usually the entertainment consisted of a hymn or two, sung by someone from another circle, or by someone's daughters. After the program, it was time to eat. For Ma--and every other member of her circle--this meant having the opportunity to consume buttered bread (both brown and white), strawberry jam, chokecherry jelly, longhorn cheese, *geitost*, a chocolate cake with white frosting, and a yellow cake with chocolate frosting, a lime gelatin salad with apples in it, and buns filled with ham salad or tuna salad. (Ma stayed away from the angel food. Mrs. Halverson was in her circle and she made the best angel food in the world. Ma knew when not to try to compete.) Ma always tried to make her table a little more special by serving little pastel-colored mints. They went so nicely with coffee.

Now, thought Karl, if Ma is going to have circle on Wednesday, she sure ain't going to be going to town. This thought cheered him as he slid the square shovel along the gutter and loaded manure into the wheelbarrow. It continued to cheer him as he put the cream into the cooler, and as he drove the cows out of the barn.

As he walked to the house, it started to rain. "Hello, *Puppen*," he said, as the dog ran up to him. "Ain't it a nice day?"

7

First Date

7

Sunset on the Minnesota prairie was a serene and restful experience. For some reason, the sun seemed to grow at about eight o'clock spreading a glow over the fields making the wheat seem more golden, and the corn and alfalfa more green, than they actually were. It was always a quiet time. One could hear cattle bawl from several farms away, punctuated by the dolorous cry of a mourning dove. The night train going through Vingelen four miles away even sounded sleepy, but Karl wasn't sleepy.

The whole scheme of using the old man's car to go to Orebro had worked out better than he had dared to hope. Ma was indeed busy with the circle, Pa was too tired from threshing to go along, and even Paul decided to stay home. It helped that Karl had told him to stay home and keep his mouth shut or he would get no more Sunday mornings in bed. The Model T ran great, or at least as well as it ever did. Karl roared around the swamp at the edge of Orebro with the engine dying down as he slowed to avoid a rabbit, but picking up as he tried to run down a gopher. On the straight stretch coming into town, the engine became more rhythmic and Karl attempted to sing along:

"And in the Senate, the other day,
What did President Coolidge say?
Bo-do-di-o, Bo-do-do-di-o-dum.
Remember Patrick Henry in that famous speech.
He said, 'Give me, Give me, Liberty or Blackbottom!'"

Hartvig Haugen, an old bachelor who lived on the edge of Orebro, looked at Karl strangely and shook his head. Karl was tempted to go straight to the Orebro Hotel, but then he remembered the cream cans and the eggs packed in the back seat and drove on to the creamery. It was a fairly simple transaction. The creamery proprietor simply put the cans on the scale, took out a sample to test for butterfat, and dumped the rest into a large vat. After grading the sample and weighing the empty cans, the proprietor did a little figuring and gave Karl the cash. Karl couldn't believe his good luck; the Orebro creamery really did pay a couple of pennies more for the cream. The eggs were the same, but at least they weren't any less. It was now a quarter to nine--just the right time to go calling.

Karl was wondering what the correct etiquette was for calling on a girl who lived in a hotel. He'd never done that before. He also wondered if he would sound too *Scandahoovian*. Once down in the cities someone had laughed at his accent. He had been in a restaurant in St. Paul and wanted to order a summer sausage sandwich and had asked the waitress for some *pølse*. She had looked at him strangely and said that they didn't have it. Karl couldn't believe that, and only after several minutes did the waitress realize what he wanted. He was absolutely abashed to discover that *pølse* was not an English word. "Maybe if yew vould have asked dat in Minneapolis," his father told him, "tey vould've understood yew. Dere are a lot of good people in Minneapolis, but St. Paul has a lot of Irish and people like dat." Karl wasn't sure what nationality the name Morrison was, but he was relatively sure it wasn't *Scandahoovian*, and she sure didn't talk like one. Maybe, he thought, that's why I like to talk to her.

Before entering the hotel Karl managed to peek in the window, and there she was! Finding a strategic observation post between two auction posters, Karl literally held his breath as he saw her. She seemed even prettier than he had remembered. She was wearing a sleeveless peach-colored dress and was casually draped across a chair reading a copy of the **Saturday Evening Post**.

Let it be understood that Karl had had his share of experiences with women. He was a twenty-three year-old Swedish-American man which meant he liked women, and assumed that women liked him, and often left it at that. Nevertheless, he had always considered himself a success with the ladies and indeed, all the girls of the Vingelen area thought him to be witty, charming, and an extremely good catch. He was always able to feel completely at ease with women his own age, and with a skill that even Paul envied, could talk to them about the most unimportant topics with complete conviction. He should have been filled with complete confidence tonight, but he wasn't.

He quickly ducked behind the darker of the two posters enabling the window to provide a reasonable mirror. He observed his hair with complete disgust. It was clean enough but he really wished he had stopped at the barber shop last Saturday night. He tried out a smile. It looked sappy. He tilted his head, trying to find a rakish angle. This maneuver enabled him to spot a rooster tail at the back of his head. He hastily dug out a comb and, like a mother cat, he licked his hand and tried to plaster down his hair. He dropped the comb and in a hurried attempt to pick it up, bumped his head on the window sill. Get ahold of yourself Karl, he said to himself. This will not do.

He looked at himself once again, ruing the unfortunate accident with the pig as he examined his nose. He shrugged and decided there was nothing to be done about his appearance at this point. He took the first two steps toward the entrance and was surprised how unsteady his knees were. His mouth was dry. The words of Reidar Simonsen came back to him: "I tell ya, it was dry as a popcorn fart." Karl grinned as he thought of it. Unknown to Karl, it was just the right kind of smile for seeing a girl whom he hoped to impress.

"Karl! I was wondering if I would ever see you again. How's your eye?" asked Julie. Karl had no doubt that she was glad to see him.

"Better for seeing you," quipped Karl, who immediately wondered if it was a dumb thing to say. "So, this is where you live."

Julie immediately rose when Karl entered. Now she stood rather awkwardly with one hand leaning on the back of the chair, and the other self-consciously running her fingers through her hair. She looked around her and admitted, "Yes, this is where I live, but only for two more nights. That's the reason I was wondering if I would see you again. You see, we are going to Vingelen for a few days."

"You are? That's great!" said Karl, and then a sudden and embarrassing silence developed. After looking at her for what seemed a very long time, Karl blurted, "Uh, er, uh, you wanna go down to Carlson's Cafe for some pop or ice cream?"

Julie could not hide her joy. "Sure. That would be nice. I'll just run up and tell Dad where I'm going."

Karl fidgeted in the lobby, standing on one foot and then the other, as he waited for Julie to return. Iver Johnson came through, carrying his drumsticks, and eyed him suspiciously. At last Julie returned and as she did, Karl noticed that she had gone to a little trouble in combing her hair and that she now looked quite stunning. Karl said, "Well, should we go then?" and inwardly cringed at the realization that it was a dumb thing to ask. When they had gone through the door and reached the sidewalk, Karl offered Julie his arm and, much to his relief, she took it.

Together they walked down the boardwalk to Carlson's Cafe. It was an unusually warm evening so, of course, that gave them something to talk about. As they eased into the cafe, Karl spotted the most isolated booth and gently guided Julie to it. He couldn't help looking around to see if Shitleg was on duty. Unfortunately he was, and Karl decided against hand-dipped ice cream. Shitleg plodded over to them and inelegantly asked, "What you want?"

Julie, who had taken a quick glance at his pants leg, replied, "I'll have a lime phosphate."

This was good news for Karl. A phosphate was only a nickel. In the manner of one who has just heard someone else order his favorite vintage, he nodded approvingly and said, "I'll have the same."

Not even Shitleg could take a long time making lime phosphates, and they soon had their orders. Karl, who felt as though he had a fur-lined mouth, gratefully took a long sip of the sticky sweet phosphate. He could contain his curiosity no longer and

72

asked, "So, you're really coming to Vingelen? What for? I mean, we'll all be glad to have you, of course, but after what you said happened to you before, I thought you'd never come back. Besides, nobody ever really comes to Vingelen unless they have to. What's up?"

"Well," Julie began, with obvious pleasure, "you might remember that I told you that Dad was getting into the movie business. He has set up some movies to be shown in Vingelen. The first show is this coming Friday night, the day after tomorrow! I'm not sure how long he intends to stay, but it probably won't be too long, judging from his other ventures."

Karl could not hide the look of amazement that came over his face and unwittingly underscored it by exclaiming, "That's amazing! That's what I came to see you about this evening. There have been posters up in Vingelen for the last couple weeks. I was going to ask you if you would care to go. Er, um, since you will be there anyway, would you care to go with me? Or maybe you have seen the show already and maybe we could do something else while you're in town."

Julie frowned and looked slightly worried. "Actually, I don't even know what the film will be about. I asked Dad and he sort of changed the subject. He always has been sort of secretive about his businesses. In fact, it was just today that I found out that we were going to Vingelen."

Ever since the subject of the movies came up, Karl was looking for an opportunity to ask the question that had been dominating all discussions in Vingelen for the past two weeks. Now, in a tone of chattiness that belied his anticipation, Karl asked, "By the way, where did you get the baby?"

A bewildered, shocked and somewhat insulted look came over Julie's face. Cautiously she asked, "What baby?"

Karl, not yet aware that his question was leading onto dangerous ground, simply replied, "The baby that your old man, er, father is giving away at the movies."

Now Julie merely looked annoyed. "What on earth are you talking about? He doesn't have a baby, and he certainly wouldn't be giving it away if he did! Giving away a baby! You're strange!"

Karl had thought of himself in different ways, but never as strange. Suddenly, however, the incongruity of the situation became obvious. He had just informed the girl of his dreams that her own father was going to give away a live baby as a door prize at a movie show. For a few seconds he sat there with a dopey expression on his face while Julie looked the other way and vigorously stirred her phosphate with a paper straw.

Finally rising to his own defense, Karl said: "Why would I make up something like that? That's what the posters all say!"

Julie was clearly shocked and was becoming angry. Her cheeks were blushing as she leaned forward challengingly, "What posters? Do you mean to say there have been posters up all this time and I only found out about it today? That can't be my father's doing. Besides, nobody would give away a baby!"

Karl tried to assume a calming air of dignity. "Well, that's what I thought. I'm only telling you what it says on the posters. All over town there are signs that say that after the movie, a live eleven-month-old baby will be given away. I had no idea that it was your father giving away the baby."

Julie placed both hands flatly on the table and pronounced, "He is not going to give away a baby."

In his own defense, Karl pursued the matter. "He sure claims he is. Do you know of anybody who wants to get rid of a baby?"

Karl had not realized how insulting this question sounded until he looked at the resentment starting to burn in Julie's green eyes. She replied disdainfully, "Of course not!"

Meanwhile, Carlson's Cafe was starting to fill up with people who had finished their Wednesday night shopping and creamery business. Shitleg was looking annoyed that they were taking up a whole booth and doing nothing but playing with virtually empty glasses. Karl, in light of the startling revelations, felt miserable. The more he thought about it, the more ludicrous the situation became. Why did he have to bring up the baby? More to the point, what could he say now to bring them back to the point where they had been before the baby had ruined everything? He opened his mouth to remark about the heat but fortunately realized, just in time, how shallow that comment was.

More than anything else, Karl wanted to take her to the movies. Perhaps they could slip out before the presentation of the door prize. As last Karl came up with an idea to try to rescue the situation. "You know," he began tentatively, "I've always heard that they have beautiful gardens behind the hotel. I've never been there. Do you suppose you could show them to me before it gets too dark?" Of course, it was a lie for Karl had seen the gardens dozens of times.

"Sure," said Julie. "I want to get out of here anyway. Mr. Carlson looks like he wants us to leave."

"Who?" asked Karl, genuinely confused. He suddenly remembered that Shitleg was really Mr. Carlson and mumbled, "Oh yeah, I guess he does." Without another word they left the cafe and walked back to the hotel.

No doubt about it. The baby story had definitely put a damper on the evening. Julie led the way past the front entrance of the hotel and alongside an exterior stairway that served as a fire escape. A white wire gate, which had unfortunately served as perch for too many sparrows, provided an entrance to the garden. A sign admonished the patrons to keep the gate closed to keep out the dogs. Naturally, it stood wide open.

There were several neat rows of zinnias and marigolds and little beds of petunias, snapdragons, and moss roses. On a bank at the edge of the little park was a bed of mixed flowers that spelled out "Orebro." In truth, it spelled out "Orebr" because most of the flowers farming last "o" had not bloomed, but everyone thought it was still nice. The night was warm, and although it was almost ten o'clock, there was still some twilight left. Julie and Karl sat down on a white painted iron bench. It would have been a wonderful place to have a pleasant and romantic chat had it not been for the mosquitoes.

The mosquitoes in Minnesota are legendary. Once or twice a year a stranger would pass through Minnesota and comment that the mosquitoes in Alaska were larger. Minnesotans, with perverse pride, would deny this, asserting that five minutes alone with the vicious vampires at sundown near a Minnesota lake would dispel any such notions. Minnesotans would condescendingly snicker when the mosquitoes of Panama were brought up, maintaining that, had the problem of malaria been caused by Minnesota mosquitoes, no canal would ever have been built. They repeated with grave voices the story of little Mary Peterson who had gone off in the woods to search for her father only to be found minutes later as a raisin-like corpse while red lipped mosquitoes voraciously searched for another victim.

Minnesota had baby mosquitoes that could be killed in hand-to-hand combat. They had yet to learn the diabolical strategy of biting and they only attacked a person's arms and neck. The veteran mosquitoes, however, knew that in the war with humans the location of the attack meant everything. Like collecting scalps, style mattered. With satanic glee, mosquitoes honed in on the back of women's knees, the part of the back that one cannot quite reach, the lone toe that managed to protrude from a sandal, or, most diabolic of all, a mocking bite right on the hand.

In the stillness behind the Orebro Hotel one could hear the mosquitoes' continual buzz and Karl knew that if he had anything to say, he had better say it fast. Hardly daring to look at her, Karl asked: "Will you still go to the movies with me in Vingelen, then?"

Julie, looking at the Orebro sign rather than at Karl, sighed, "Yes, I suppose, but I would think the question is, would you still want to go with me? Why, oh why, does my father do things like this? Maybe he has some idea of getting revenge against Vingelen for what happened last time. At least we will be staying in a hotel this time. But, I mean, a baby! What can he have in mind? Anyway, if this is going to be one of Dad's schemes, I may just need your protection. What time is the movie supposed to start?"

"Uh, well, uh, the poster says it will start at 8:30."

Julie smiled and self-consciously straightened her skirt. "I think, all things considered, I'd like to go with you very much. Why don't you come by the hotel about eight o'clock. Maybe I'll know more about the baby then."

"Sure. Sounds great!" All this time Karl had been inching his arm along the back of the bench. Now he gently but firmly squeezed her shoulder and moved his face closer to hers. He was pleasantly surprised to see how little she resisted and before he had time to worry about what he would do next, he was kissing her gently on the lips. She returned the kiss with what Karl judged was a great reciprocity of feeling.

Karl was overcome by an awareness of what he was doing. Hey, he thought, I'm really kissing her. The prettiest girl I ever met, and I'm actually kissing her. Not only that, but she is kissing me back. Ummmm, is she ever kissing me back. I could spend the rest of my life kissing her. I want to spend the rest of my life kissing her.

Julie's mind was racing. Her eyes were closed tightly as she thought, I've never met a man like you, Karl. I wanted you to do this ever since the first time I saw you. I hope you don't think I'm too easy. This is really only the first time we have been alone together. But don't stop. I could go on like this forever. What am I doing? Karl is a farmer! I don't want to get involved with a farmer! I....

At that moment, Julie opened her eyes. "Karl," she whispered, "do you know that your nose..."

Karl abruptly sat up, and with a voice filled with shame and disgust, said "I know, I know. It's horribly bent and crooked. I didn't mean for it to get in the way. I broke it in an accident and that's just the way it healed. I'm sorry."

Julie laughed, which made Karl even more embarrassed. "No, no Karl. I had never noticed that. I just wanted to tell you that your nose is being bitten by a mosquito."

Karl reached up and squashed the mosquito. His nose was now plastered with a nasty smudge of the late insect and a small pool of blood. Karl didn't care. Neither did Julie. Karl moved in for another kiss. But the spell was broken and the pleasant confusion caused by kissing a lovable farmer was such that Julie abruptly stood up and said, "I suppose we had better go in. I'm getting eaten up by these mosquitoes, too."

Damn the mosquitoes! thought Karl, but he gallantly said, "Of course." Yet neither of them wanted to make the first step of retreat.

Karl gently put his arm around Julie's waist as she leaned tenderly against him. Both were silently aware of their closeness and intimacy and both enjoyed it immensely even though Karl's other arm was constantly waving at mosquitoes. Julie lightly slapped Karl's cheek, and for a moment he wondered if his hand had been somewhere it shouldn't have been. Julie, however, immediately said, "I'm sorry I didn't see him sooner. Now there's blood on your cheek as well as on your nose. Your brother will think you've been in a fight."

Karl sighed and smiled ingratiatingly as he said, "Well, I think I'll just let him think so." To himself Karl thought, like heck I will. I can hardly wait to get home to tell him I've been kissing the prettiest girl either of us has ever seen.

He was delighted to find the lobby of the hotel deserted and was actually licking his lips in anticipation of a good night kiss. He took both of Julie's hands and was in the process of drawing her near when Iver Johnson, oblivious to the tender moment unfolding before him, stood up from behind the couch and joyously announced, "Ah, I thought I heard somebody come in. Hey, you're that oldest Thorson kid, ain't you? Come here a minute. I got the damnedest thing to show you."

The hotel proprietor led them behind the leather sofa and said, "Here. Get down on your knees and look in there. D'you see that? It's a mouse nest. I got a whole family of mice in my couch. Kind of cute, ain't they?"

Julie, who had been sitting in that couch every day since coming to Orebro, stifled a scream. She had once mentioned to Iver that noises seemed to be coming from the couch, but he had assured her that all leather couches squeaked. She shuddered now and whispered to Karl, "Does the Vingelen Hotel cater with such hospitality to rodents?"

They shared one more laugh and then smiled into each other's eyes. Karl risked one quick kiss while Iver was preoccupied with the mice and then reluctantly said, "Well, I'll see you the day after tomorrow then. About eight?"

Julie squeezed his hand and said, "Yes. I'll be looking for you."

Karl floated back to where he had left the Model T. He kept telling himself that he was not a kid and should display a mature demeanor. But he grinned a lot and had to fight off an urge to run. Karl Thorson had never been in love before. He wondered if he was now. He decided that maybe he was.

At that very moment, back on the farm, Pa blew out the lamp and climbed into bed next to Ma. For as long as they had been married, Pa had always slept on the right side of the bed and Ma on the left side. Only once in their marriage had this not occurred. About a dozen years earlier, they had retired at their usual hour and Ma, whose side of the bed was next to the window, had carefully pulled down the shade. Three hours later, she was jarred awake by the sound of breaking glass. Something had crashed through the window. Pa nervously lit the lamp only to have the light reveal a horse's rear end. Pa thought it was sort of funny, and made some comment about Republicans coming to visit, but Ma was screaming. It seemed that the horse had merely gotten loose and found the flowers near the house to be irresistible.

Unfortunately, the matter had not ended there. When they had tied up the horse, picked up the glass, and were ready to retire again, a bat flew into the room. Ma hated bats, and began to scream. Pa hated bats even more and was terrified of them, but with difficulty he refrained from screaming. They just *knew* that bats would try to make nests in their hair. Karl was eleven years old at the time and, awakened by his mother's screams, came down from his upstairs room in time to see Ma and Pa on the end of a broom handle that had been inserted in a crack of the doorway. There they blindly waved the broom in an attempt to kill the bat. Karl thought it looked like fun and a grabbed towel and a frying pan. In a matter of seconds he tossed the towel over the bat and pounded it into a bloody, squeaky, and decidedly nasty, pulp. As Ma was panting and Pa was looking pale, Karl scooped it up and flung it outside for a lucky cat. Ma insisted that the bed be moved next to the wall where she slept all night with the covers over her head.

Now, Pa was chuckling to himself and finally remarked, "Vell, I hope Karl had a good time tonight."

Ma, never known for her perception, continued to stare at the ceiling and said with real concern, "Yes, it would be nice to get a few pennies more for the cream. I don't know what we are going to do if prices don't go up pretty soon. I had thought that maybe even one day we could get a radio, but I don't see how we can do it now."

She became aware that the bed was shaking from Pa's silent giggling and she rather indignantly asked, "What's so funny about us being too poor to afford a radio?"

"It's you, Ma. Yew really tink Karl vas so anxious to go to Orebro yust to get a few more cents for da cream? He's going sparking. Didn't yew see how dressed up he vas. He looked yust like me ven I vent out to court my little Norvegian girl."

That put them both in a tender mood, and Ma snuggled closer to Pa. But Pa was turning serious. "Yew know, Ma, I tink it's a good ting, tew. Karl needs to get out on his own. I only vish dat I had something tew give him. Maybe I should yust give him da farm. He's a good kid, and I always been so proud of him; but I don't know, sometimes it's like he needs a kick in da pants or someting. Yew know vat I really tink it is, he yust doesn't vant to leave me vit all da vork. Paul, he'll be all right, he vants to get out of here as soon as he can and vork on cars. Dere's good money in dat. But Karl, vell, I tink da first ting he needs is a good woman to help him decide vat he vants to do."

Ma raised herself on one elbow and said, "But do you know anything about this girl? Do you think she's Lutheran?"

8

Hollywood Comes
to Vingelen

8

It hadn't rained for several days and the Model T raised a towering cloud of dust as Paul and Karl drove to Vingelen. There had been no realistic way of getting rid of Paul. He wanted to see the movie as much as Karl did and even hoped that he might find a girl there, too. Ma and Pa even wanted to come along at first, but Karl was able to talk them out of it. In the midst of his thinking about Julie, Karl kept telling himself that one day soon he would just have to get a car of his own.

They had finished threshing at the Peterson place the day before and, as usual, the last crop at the Henrickson farm wasn't ready yet. Karl was able to take his time getting "spiffed up" and was pleased with the effect. Paul couldn't help but notice that Karl looked a little better then he usually did for going into town. As they drove along, Karl was moved to song.

> Yes, We have no bananas...
> We have no bananas today.
> We've peaches & onions & rye bread & *lefse*
> And all kinds of fruit and thiinnggss.
>
> But, yes, We have no bananas...
> We have no bananas today.

Paul, who insisted on driving, had had enough. "Why don't you learn the words to a song. Of course they wouldn't have *lefse*! What kind of a store would have *lefse*? By the way, you sure seem confident tonight. What if she decided not to come along with her old man? The way you look and smell, you're sure to get picked up by some female--maybe even one with two legs."

Karl was too elated to think of an appropriately vulgar retort. That very afternoon Pa, who seemed to know a whole lot more about things than he could reasonably be expected to, had slipped a dollar bill into Karl's shirt just as Karl was ready to take a load of wheat into the elevator in Vingelen. With a fatherly smile he told Karl, "If you're goin' sparkin', den I tink yew could use a new shirt."

Karl's first instinct had been to deny that he was going sparking, but for once he was able to act nonchalantly and merely said, "Hey, thanks Pa. I can use a new shirt." He briefly admired himself in the mirror before leaving the house and decided his appearance was just about the best he could do. With this self assurance, he told his brother, "Now, now, just because you don't have a date, Paul, there's no sense in being jealous of those of us who are more charming. Besides, Pa said I had to put gas in the car and I'm not even asking you to pay your share. Stick with me, little brother-- but not too close--and you might learn something."

"If I did, it would be the first time," said Paul.

There were already several cars in town by the time they reached Vingelen and Karl had to park in front of Nelson's Store. This somewhat dismayed Karl because as he got out of the car, everyone noticed that he was dressed for courting. Karl, in spite of self-assurance, blushed.

The Vingelen Hotel was not as large or imposing as the Orebro Hotel. It was made of wood and looked like just another large house. It was clean and well run with a large porch that extended all along the south wall. The porch was furnished with two old church pews. The effect might have been better had the pews come from the same church, but they provided seating for at least seven potential guests who might be interested in the goings on of Main Street in Vingelen. Karl never had many occasions to enter the hotel but when he did he was drawn to the registration table. It had fascinated him ever since he first saw it as a boy. It was a round, darkly varnished oak table with legs that seemed to be made out of eagle's legs. Each set of talons held a glass ball about the size of an orange. When he first saw it Karl promised himself that he would get a table like that when he grew up. He thought about that now. "Well, here I am, all grown up and I still don't have an eagle-claw table. I wonder if they would ever sell it. Karl needed to think of something. He knew he was acting nervous and his hands felt moist. I feel like a thirteen year old, he thought. Still, what's wrong with that? I guess it feels sort of nice.

Across the street from the hotel was a large vacant lot that was a swamp when it rained, and a parking lot when it didn't. Tonight it was already filling up with cars, mostly Model T's. Karl walked up to the porch and self-consciously nodded to two old men who were speaking Norwegian and chewing *snus*. He knew that neither one of them stayed at the hotel, but it was a nice place to sit on a summer's night.

Julie was waiting for him when he entered the lobby. He was relieved, because he didn't know what he would have done if she hadn't been. Nevertheless, he temporarily forgot to breathe. She was wearing a rather simple lime green dress that brought out the emerald richness of her eyes. Her skillful use of rouge highlighted her cheeks and made the rest of her face glow against the dark outline of her hair. Karl tried to talk but was forced to clear his throat before he was able to gasp out, "There's still some time left before the pictures are suppose to start. How about coming down to the Castle Garden Inn with me?" Julie said, "All right" and slipped her arm in his.

Walking down the boardwalk toward the Castle Garden Inn with an unfamiliar beautiful girl on his arm made Karl just a little self-conscious. He knew everyone in town was watching and wondering who she was. He was glad. Just to be chatty, Karl asked, "By the way, what is the title of the movie that your father is showing tonight? The posters never said."

Julie frowned.

"I asked my father that. He said that the first one was called **Gold of the Yukon**." Then I asked my father, "You mean there will be more than one?" and he said, "Oh yes, there will be several."

"What are the other ones called?" asked Karl, with genuine interest.

"Well, that's the funny thing. He said he didn't know what the other ones were called. Oh Karl, I'm worried. Not only does he refuse to tell me what this baby business is all about, but he doesn't seem to have the slightest idea of how to show movies. He just came back from Fargo on the train today with five reels of film. Ever since he got back he has been running all over town to see if he can find someone who knows how to run a movie projector."

"Who did he find?"

Julie raised her eyebrows in supplication. "As of an hour ago, nobody!"

There already was a good crowd at the Castle Garden Inn. Karl and Julie took the only booth left, the one right by the door. Karl regretted the lack of privacy. He had good reason to, for as soon as they sat down, Reidar Simonsen came over and looked down on Julie with his perpetual smirk. "Well Karl, who do we have here?"

"Uh, Julie Morrison, I'd like you to meet Reidar Simonsen," Karl mumbled.

"Morrison! No relation to that guy whose wagon we shoved in the lake a couple of years ago, I hope. Heh, heh, remember that Karl, how..."

"Yes," Karl hurriedly interjected, "I do remember when that unfortunately happened..."

"Unfortunately?" asked Reidar with a puzzled expression.

"and I'd like you know that Julie *is* Mr. Morrison's daughter," said Karl.

Julie was sputtering, "So you are one of those animals that pushed the wagon into the lake. I happened to be in that wagon, and I swore that if I ever found out who did it I'd, I'd, I'd..."

"Julie, please," interjected Karl, "that was a long time ago and I'm sure that Reidar and anyone else who was involved in that is sorry for it now. Aren't THEY, Reidar?" Those words, along with the cold stare, were enough to send Reidar the messages that Julie did not know that Karl had helped push the wagon and that he had no intention of telling her. Reidar quickly apologized.

"Hey, I'm really sorry to hear you were in the wagon. None of us would have done it if we had known that you were in there. Really. Uh, you know, we were just kids and it seemed like an innocent stunt." Reidar grinned broadly and added, "I'm sure *everybody* involved would like to apologize to you."

Eager to change the subject, Karl said, "Julie's father is presenting the movies tonight."

"No kidding! Where did he get the eleven-month-old baby he's giving away?" asked Reidar.

"Really," Julie said with a trace of exasperation, "I don't know anything about it. I've never seen any baby. Are you going to be at the show?"

"Sure. Wouldn't miss it. I hope your father doesn't have any hard feelings about what happened a couple of years ago. This really is a nice town, you know, " Reidar assured her.

"I'm sure he's forgotten all about it," Julie lied.

Reidar considered himself to be sufficiently ingratiated and sat down with them and ordered three cups of coffee. Weather served as a suitable conversational topic followed by a few observations about how Vingelen was a much nicer town than Orebro. Before long it was time to go to the theater.

The Vingelen Theater was a pride and joy of the town. It was one of the larger buildings in town and, constructed as it was out of cement blocks, one of Vingelen's most permanent buildings. It was equipped with fold-up wooden seats which could be removed for any number of functions. The walls, curiously, were of white painted plaster and while this rather interfered with the necessary darkness of a projection room, it did help the people find their seats easily. Julie and Karl, arriving early, took seats in the center.

It soon became obvious that, baby or not, this was not going to be a commercial success. Karl had assumed that everybody in town would be there. At least, everybody had been talking about the baby. True, many of the people had talked with disgust about giving away a baby, but matters of taste had never kept people away before. Yet, it was a busy time of the year. Most people were still threshing and there were long lines at both of the grain elevators.

Sigurd Nelson and Charlie Holm were already in the theater, and Paul soon came in with the Andersson brothers. They all looked at Karl, and especially at Julie. Paul walked up to Julie and said, "Hi. Remember me?"

"Of course. You're Karl's brother, Paul. You were with Karl at the dance in Orebro."

"That's right. Welcome to Vingelen," said Paul, grandly. "I see your father got someone to run the projector."

"Oh, yeah?" Karl interrupted, "Who did he get?"

"John Bunge," sniggered Paul.

"Oh God no! Not John. What does he know about it? I doubt if he has ever seen a movie."

Karl could see trouble ahead. John Bunge averaged three permanent jobs a year, and was currently ruining engines at the gas station.

"Charlie just talked to him," added Paul. "He claims he's getting a dollar an hour but he would probably do it for free if he got to draw the name for the baby winner."

It was already twenty minutes past the time when the show was supposed to start and it was obvious that the theater would not even be half full. After a few rude catcalls, the lights were turned off and the movie began. The screen came to life with the title *Stagecoach to Deadwood*.

"I thought you said that it was going to be *Gold of the Yukon*," whispered Karl.

"That's what father told me," replied Julie, in a note of real terror. "Maybe the wrong film got into the box."

"That's alright," said Karl. "*Stagecoach to Deadwood* sounds just as good." He couldn't help realizing how condescending this sounded.

The crowd, or at least what there was of it, settled back to enjoy the film. Karl had to admit it was better than he had expected. John Bunge, it seemed, really did know how to run a projector. A five-reeler meant that it would be a nice long film. Karl thought he might try to put his arm around Julie in about the third reel. By that time the adventure, already going great guns, ought to be at its height. Black Bart had learned about the huge gold shipment that was about to leave Deadwood. He had selected a perfect spot for an ambush. A huge cloud of dust indicated that the stage was just around the bend. Black Bart took out his six-guns. The screen went white.

"Not bad, huh?" Karl called to Paul, who sat three rows ahead of him. "Think he'll get away with it in the next reel?"

"He might," answered Paul, "But I think the marshall already suspects him."

Turning back to Julie who was looking somewhat relieved, Karl said, "Your father has really got something here. Do you think this will be his career now?"

"I hope so," Julie answered, "It's about time he finds something permanent and he seems real excited about this. I wish I could enjoy it more, though. I keep thinking about that eleven-month-old baby."

Shortly afterwards the lights were turned off again, and the audience looked forward to the resumption of *Stagecoach to Deadwood*. The screen was filled with the words, *Gold of the Yukon*. Various voices could be heard.

"What happened to the cowboys?"

"Bring back Black Bart."

"I knew Bunge would screw it up!"

Julie held her face in her hands. "I knew it. I knew it. I knew it. Just once why couldn't things have gone right?"

Karl tried to reassure her. "Settle down. I'm sure it will be all right. Bunge just got the reels mixed up, that's all. It's fine. This way we will get to see two movies. Nobody is going to blame your father for this."

Gold of the Yukon was indeed an engrossing film. John Bunge kept it rolling, and before long people had all but forgotten about *Stagecoach to Deadwood*. Dawson Dick had left the Widow Morgan alone in the line shack while he went for help. The snow became heavier as Dick tried to cross the treacherous river. His dog team refused to budge but when Dick cracked his whip, they ran yelping across the ice. Suddenly the ice cracked and they tilted dangerously. The first reel of *Gold of the Yukon* had ended.

Karl and Julie sat there without talking. Both were afraid of what would be on the next reel. Would it be *Gold of the Yukon* or *Stagecoach to Deadwood*. The people around them seemed to want to find out what happened to Dawson Dick more than Black Bart. The more Karl thought about it, the more logical--even ingenious--the whole thing seemed to be.

"'Ya know, I got to hand it to your father. That's really pretty clever to show two films like this. It gives you two plots to follow and really keeps you interested. I wonder why none of the movie houses in Fargo have ever done this. *Ja*, I think he's pretty clever."

Julie smiled and seemed somewhat reassured. The lights went off and the projector danced to life filling the screen with *Florida's Everglades*. This time nobody said a word. They seemed to think they had figured out the system. A five-reel film meant showing half of one picture, half of another, then a nice travelogue, followed by the second halves of the feature films. It had a certain logic to it, or at least it seemed to. Still, nobody felt relaxed about it, least of all, Julie. Karl decided that he wouldn't try to put his arm around her on the third reel. After a surfeit of flamingos and alligators, the lights again came on. The theater was remarkably silent.

The wait for the fourth reel seemed interminable. Karl fidgeted and Julie twisted a handkerchief in her hands. Paul and the Andersson boys seemed embarrassed to look their way. At last the lights were again turned off. This time there were no titles of any kind, only an abrupt resumption of action. It was the action of the Keystone Kops. Several people now booed. Reidar Simonsen cheered. A fourteen-year-old boy threw an apple core at the screen and demanded the return of the cowboys. Yet, curiously, nobody left the theatre.

Nobody, that is, except Julie. When Karl turned to express his sympathy for her embarrassment, he was startled to see that she had disappeared. Karl got up to find her, but realized that he wouldn't know what to say if he did find her, so he slumped back into his chair. He didn't think that the Keystone Kops were particularly funny that evening and it didn't even surprise him that the fifth reel was a middle reel from something about Louis XIII and the Three Musketeers. He had even forgotten about the baby.

However, when the lights came on, it was clear that the rest of the audience had not forgotten the baby. They had each paid the outrageous price of a dollar to see five unconnected and irrelevant pieces of film, and now they demanded that their curiosity about the baby be satisfied. An air of almost ghoulish expectation settled over the theater. At last Doc Morrison made his way to the front of the theater and stood before the screen.

He looked much the same as two years ago when Karl had seen him peddling elixir, but now Karl looked for some resemblance of Julie in his face. Karl decided they had the same coloring, but other than that there was not much to indicate that they were father and daughter. Morrison's eyes seemed to have acquired a shiftier look and although it was not particularly warm in the theater, he was sweating profusely. Most people noticed immediately that he was carrying neither a box of signed ticket stubs nor a baby.

"May I have your attention, please," he began. "I regret' to inform you that because of the poor attendance tonight I will not be able to hold the drawing for the eleven-month-old baby. Tonight's attendance has been so low that I have not been able to cover my considerable expenses in raising the infant to its present age. Therefore, I have decided to postpone the drawing until tomorrow night. You have all been treated to some of the finest film that Hollywood has to offer..."

At this he was interrupted by hoots and groans. "...and so I ask that you tell your friends to come here tomorrow night at which time I am sure attendance will be such that I will be able to proceed with the drawing. I also invite you to come back tomorrow since for obvious reasons, it would be unfair to those coming tomorrow to include your entries in the drawing. By coming tomorrow night, you will have an equal chance of winning a fine baby. Until then, as they say in your fine community, '*Gud vell.*'" (His Norwegian pronunciation of "good evening" was more puzzling than polite.)

He was gone in a minute. The audience, poorer but wiser,

drifted out. They all felt cheated, but mostly because they didn't get a chance to see the baby. Paul saw that Karl was alone and quickly caught up to him.

"Where's Julie?"

Karl was clearly disgusted and seemed to sneer as he said, "I don't know. She left sometime during the fourth reel. I suppose I should go to the hotel and see if I can cheer her up. I dunno, what can I say? The old *dritsek* has done it again!" (A *dritsek* was an uncomplimentary term meaning literally a bag of manure.)

Paul went with Karl to the hotel. To no one's surprise, Julie refused to see anyone. They walked slowly along the boardwalk and crossed the street to the Castle Garden Inn. The usual gang was there and although it was evident that they had been talking in quite heated tones about the movie and the lack of the drawing, they now became politely silent and shared Karl's embarrassment.

Charlie Holm seemed especially sympathetic. "'Ya get to talk to her, then? She didn't look too happy at the end of the third reel."

"Nah, and I can't blame her none," admitted Karl. "She was so worried something like this would happen. I tell 'ya, she didn't know anything about it."

"*Ja*, that's too bad," said Clare Andersson.

"It sure is," added Swen Sandquist who hadn't been there but had just heard all about it.

"*Ja*, it's a shame, that's for sure," said Knut Andersson who could not conceal the giggle in his voice.

"Well, are you going to go again tomorrow night?" asked Charlie with a silly smirk on his face.

Karl saw nothing amusing about the situation. "I'll probably never see her again. But gol-dang it, it ain't her fault that her old man's a crook."

At that, nobody could think of much to say except to agree that Julie's old man was a crook and that it was hardly her fault. Paul suggested that they go home and Karl was only too glad to leave. He had not planned to be riding around in the Model T with his brother at this time of night, and he blamed Paul for *making* him go to the dance in Orebro in the first place.

9

Daddy's Girl

9

Saturday mornings in Vingelen were always very quiet. No one from the farms ever came into town on Saturday mornings, lest they would lose their excuse for coming in on Saturday night. Threshing wouldn't began until all the dew was off the shocks so there were no lines of grain wagons at the elevators. Other than a chirping robin, not a single sound came to Julie's ears as she stared out the window looking down on Main Street. She had gone to bed the night before soon after she had returned from the Vingelen Theater. She couldn't bear to talk to her father, and when he at last came in (she could easily identify his tread on the creaky hotel stairs), she had pretended to be asleep.

But she had stayed awake for hours. It had been warm in her room so she had kept the window open. She could hear every word of those who passed by as they discussed the movies, her father, and the baby. She desperately wanted sleep to come, but she couldn't control her thoughts which ran in a zig-zag course from the past to the future. The past was too depressing; the future too hopeless.

Frogs croaked in the slough across the street. A cricket seemed to be trapped somewhere inside her room. The only light came from the moon filtered through thin curtains. Julie stared at the dim red and yellow roses in the wallpaper. Here I am, she told herself, in Vingelen, Minnesota! Everything I have in the world is in that one cardboard suitcase at my aunt's place. I wonder how much of that psychology stuff I read about in *Collier's* magazine is true? Especially the bit about your possessions revealing your personality. If that's true, I have no personality unless you consider four dresses, two pairs of shoes, some underwear and a purse holding nineteen dollars and eighty-five cents a personality!

I'll never see Karl again. By now he has also realized this and probably thinks he is pretty lucky not to have gotten involved any further with me. Maybe I do too. What would it have been like to be married to Karl, anyhow? He would have continued to be a farmer, I suppose, which would have made me a farmer's wife. Shudder! We would have lived out in the country with a dog and cats and pigs and chickens and horses and cows--all of which would have to be fed by someone--most likely me. I suppose I would have to learn to milk cows. I bet I could do it, too. But, those cows would be better to work with than Mrs. Roberts on Lake Street. I never want to be a maid again!

I suppose the big social event of the week would be going to this stupid village on Saturday night and drinking coffee at the Castle Garden Inn. What a dumb name for a cafe. Then, of course, there would be church on Sunday out in the country. I wonder what goes on inside a Lutheran Church? I suppose Karl is a Lutheran. It can't be that much different from being Methodist. I mean, it wouldn't be like marrying a Catholic or anything. Dad was upset when I just went to a dance with that Paul Kelly even though I liked him. Maybe I would have married Karl even if he were a Catholic. Who was that King of France we read about in school, the one who was a Protestant and became a Catholic to get the crown and said, 'Paris is worth a mass?' Louis the...uh–uh...no - Henry IV, that's it. I could be like Henry IV. I wonder if Karl likes history? He talks like he is pretty well read.

Oh why am I thinking about him? What about Dad? What about me? Where do we go from here? When do we go from here? I have a feeling that when we do go, it had better be fast. I must have it out with him. When we left Minneapolis he said it would only be a matter of time before we would settle permanently and he would have a "position!" I suppose he was probably telling the truth. He never claimed that a matter of time would be soon.

But this baby business. He must have some plan to get out of

it, and it better be good enough to soothe the tempers of these people. If the movie would have been any good, he might have gotten
away with it. I got the feeling that the locals were actually grateful
to him for bringing some entertainment into this town; but this,
this baby farce! Those people are already in an ugly mood.
What's it going to be like if he pulls the same trick tonight? At the
very least, he owes me an explanation. I can't let him ruin my
future and I can't become party to a swindle. Tomorrow-- the first
thing tomorrow-- we are going to have it out!

Julie made this resolve several times during the course of the
next three hours. In between, her mind wandered from her immediate past to her immediate future and she was dissatisfied with
both. Perhaps because the present was so dismal, she increasingly
thought of the more pleasant times of childhood and just when she
thought she would never go to sleep, she did.

Now it was morning and she dressed in one of her four dresses that defined her personality-- modern, tasteful, and unique for
Vingelen-- as she watched her father leave the Castle Garden Inn,
where he had enjoyed a particularly tasty breakfast, and amble
back to the hotel. As she watched him return, Julie mentally
rehearsed her speech. It was time to have it out.

Doc Morrison was pleased with himself. Not a bad take last
night. I can do this show two or three times a week in every town
in the Red River Valley. Maybe I'll buy a car. Hey, maybe I'll
even buy a baby to give away. Ah, the farmer, God love 'em. God
love 'em because I sure don't, but my, oh my, do they provide a
fine crop at this time of the year. God would not have given us
sheep if he did not intend them to be fleeced. Next week I think
I'd better give some town in North Dakota a try. I'd better check
the train schedules this afternoon. With the profits from last night
I think I might celebrate by buying myself a new tie.

Morrison never went anywhere without a tie. He had had the
same suit for three years and anyone who could get past looking at
his tie would have noticed that the suit was also due for replacement. Few people ever got past his ties, however. He prided himself on having one for each day of the week. Today's was yellow.
It was not a wise choice. Morrison avoided the direct rays of the

sun whenever possible and the result was a pale and sallow complexion that did not exactly complement his cadaverous eyes. He was only forty-two years old, but graying hair and a thin graying mustache made him appear at least ten years older. He could have made a career as a salesman had he been able to keep his eyes on the person he was, but Morrison was always shifting his gaze giving him a furtive, even sneaky, look. In an occupation where being memorable is not always a prime asset, Morrison was memorable. His height, weight, and general demeanor were all supreme examples of calculated ordinariness, but his tie and sneaky eyes were unforgettable. His ego, undeflated by years of business and social failures, would not permit him to slouch so over the years he had acquired a curious little strut that kept his nose in the air and his eyes moving constantly. As one Vingelen resident would later say, "He always seemed to have one eye out for birds."

Now, as he climbed the stairs of the Vingelen Hotel, he told himself that this life was really unfair to Juliette. I've got to find her a place to stay. Besides, in this movie racket she is somewhat of a liability. I might have to move quickly some day and she would get in the way. I'd miss her though, and who else would put up with me? I promised Helen I'd take care of her and by God, I will. As soon as I get enough money to set myself up, I can have a good home for her and then she'll meet some decent Romeo. One thing for sure-- I ain't going to have her marry one of these farmers. My little girl deserves better than that. Helen would turn over in her grave if I let her marry one of these rubes.

He entered his room to find Julie waiting for him. "'Morning, Juliette. Have you had any breakfast yet? I was just down at the Castle Garden Inn. Ordered the flapjacks. Best I ever ate." Morrison was aware that his cheerfulness sounded faked. Ever since he had seen Julie run out of the theater the night before, he had been dreading speaking to her. Now he could see in her eyes that a showdown of some sort was in the making. "Er, ah, anything wrong?"

"You know perfectly well there is. Last night I went to the movies thinking that at last my father was in a business I could be proud of and I was sitting there with a man that I was fond of. I wanted him to think I came from normal parentage and I wanted him to think that I was like other girls he might have known. But no, I have to have a father who promises to give away live babies, and one who shows pointless and stupid reels from different movies. That smacks of a swindle. I refuse to be a part of it. Ever since Mama died you have been moving from one shady deal to another. You drag me around with you. Why? What am I supposed to do? Provide you with a smokescreen of respectability? I won't do it any longer. I'm not going to be an accomplice to a swindle, and when you promise to give away a live baby and obviously don't have one, that is a swindle! I thought the eyeglass business was bad. Next you played upon the fears of all those dumb farmers and sold them lightning rods. But this! This sordid promise to give away a baby at a picture show, that in itself is a fraud! Well, you've outdone yourself."

"I love you," Julie quickly added. "In spite of everything, I love you. But I won't go out on the road with you ever again. If we can't live in a real home, I'm going back to the cities and get a job as a maid or something. Of course, because I've been traipsing around the country with you, I don't know the first thing about housework. I found that out last time I tried it, but I'd rather be humiliated daily by some rich old Minneapolis woman than be humiliated before someone as decent as Karl Thorson."

Doc Morrison visibly sneered as he said, "Thorson, huh? Is that the Romeo you were sitting next to last night? Looked like a farmer. You ought to thank me."

Julie was not in a mood to be grateful. She blurted out what came to her mind which was, "How can I thank you for embarrassing me in front of the man I was going to marry?" Julie knew it was untrue. She just wanted to hurt her father but as she stood there trembling with rage in a room that seemed unnaturally silent, she began to think it might be true after all.

"So that's the way it is, huh? Well, Juliette, it is indeed time we got a few things straight around here. You think your father is no good now, huh? Now you're ashamed of him, huh? How many days have you gone hungry since your mother died? None. That's how many! I take you to Minneapolis and clerk in a department store so you can graduate from high school. How many girls in this town do you think have a high school education, huh? Now you think you're grown up enough to sit in judgment of your father and be embarrassed by him while sitting next to some farmer who was sucker enough to buy a ticket to the movie? What gives you such special insight that you think the fleecee is smarter than the fleecer?"

"And let me tell you something else," Morrison continued. "I had intended to show a real movie. I really had. But when I was in Fargo, these were the only cans of film they would sell me-- for the amount of money I had, of course. I didn't know they didn't go together until last night. I was almost as disappointed as you were. In this business, you roll with the punches. I show these films a few more times and maybe I can afford to buy some real movies. And about that baby-- that's just to get their attention. Nobody, not even these dumb farmers, can expect me to give away a real baby, can they? Besides, I got a way around that and will use it if and when I have to. But, that's my business. In the meantime, you better have some faith in your old man."

Julie shouted back, "Have you ever given me reason to?"

The moment it was out of her mouth she regretted saying it. A strange, almost dazed, hurt look spread across his face. They had been arguing almost face to face in the middle of the room, but Morrison now turned and slowly walked over to the window. As he gazed out on Main Street of Vingelen, Julie could hear his short rapid breathing and see the muscles of his neck quiver. Julie sat on the bed staring down at the faded brown and yellow rug that clashed so hideously with the blue curtains. So now I've hurt his feelings. So what! He deserves it! And it's true! Why should I have any faith in him? It's all his fault that I am sitting in this horrid room in this horrid town. Why doesn't he say something? All I can hear is that clock down in the lobby on that monstrously ugly table with the eagle-claw legs. Who would ever bring anything like that into their house? Who would be dumb enough to feature that thing in their lobby? People who would be taken in by my father the crook, that's who! I hope he isn't waiting for me to say anything. I'm not going to let him put on a martyr act so I feel guilty when I'm not to blame. Let him suffer. Let him stare out the window all day. He's had this coming for a long time. Julie found herself choking back tears and saying, "Daddy, I'm sorry."

Morrison continued to look out the window. As Julie watched, his shoulders-- perennially thrust back in an aggressive, even pompous manner-- gradually sagged and he seemed to get smaller. Finally he turned to her. The sunlight reflecting off of the glass top of the dresser made his eyes glow through the liquid of tears. She had never seen him like this.

Morrison's first words were whispered and the rest were spoken in a cracked voice. "No, Julie. I'm sorry. I'm sorry for many things. First of all, I'm sorry that I embarrassed you in front of your Romeo, er, that young man. I'm also sorry that I made light of it. It was a very selfish thing for me to do and showed an utter lack of sensitivity. Finally, and most importantly, I'm sorry for the mess I've made of your life by dragging you around the country when I should have provided a steady home for you and given you the advantages of a community and friends. All of these things were within my control and in all I have failed you."

Morrison soberly repeated these last words. His throat was dry and he wished he were somewhere else, but he knew that he would have to go on. He walked, almost stumbling, over to the pitcher of water on the dresser, drank one glass, and then another. With a different stride, one that wasn't a strut but one filled with determination, he returned to the bed where Julie was now sitting. He sat down beside Julie and took her hands in his. "I'm sorry for one other thing, Julie; I'm sorry that I haven't talked to you or trusted in your capacity to make important judgments on your own. I've been afraid to let you grow up."

Julie had never heard her father talk like this. Even when they were alone, he had always sounded like he was trying to sell something. In a timid and amazed voice she asked, "Afraid to let me grow up?"

Now, strangely confident, Morrison went on. "Do you remember what I was doing when your mother died? You were only nine then; ten years ago next Thursday to be exact, and we were living in Mayville, North Dakota. Sure I was a salesman then too, but it was a different life. I represented a real company with a good product and a good reputation. I sold the best cream separator in the world. Farmers thanked me for selling it to them. I led the company in sales for the whole state. Sure we moved around a lot even then, but usually not more than once a year. When Helen died, there was just me and you. I don't know. I guess I just didn't feel that I was able to take care of a nine-year-old girl all by myself. I loved you Julie. I loved you not only because you were my little girl, but because you were a part of Helen, and I missed her very much. I gave up my job and we moved in with your aunt because I thought you needed a woman in the house. I took a job in a department store, and while it didn't pay very much, the job had a future and I was in line to become an assistant manager. Do you remember how you used to visit me at work and we tried on shoes we could not afford?"

In a rare show of affection, Julie hugged her father's arm and said, "Yes, Daddy, I do. I loved those trips to the store."

Morrison continued, as a note of bitterness came into his voice, "Yeah, well, then the war came along. If I had been a farmer or something I maybe could have gotten out of it. I certainly didn't volunteer, that's for sure. But what could I do? Somebody drew my name out of a hat or something, and the next thing I knew, I was ordered to go to camp. Almost two years out of my life. Almost two years without seeing the only person I really cared about in my life. And when I came back, you were twelve years old."

"The war changed me. In fact, it changed everybody who was in it. I'm not bellyaching about a country ignoring its heroes. I wasn't a hero. None of the guys I knew acted liked heroes. I was in Ardennes with a million other guys. I shot my gun in the general direction of the Germans, but I doubt that I ever hit anyone. In fact, I hope I didn't. Apparently enough guys did, though, because we won and we sort of thought we were making the world safe for democracy. I suppose as much as anything, I thought I was making a better world for you. We all had plans about how we were going to go back home and pick up our lives where they had left

102

off."

A heavy silence, broken only by the sound of a mail cart being pushed toward the depot, settled back over the sunny room. Morrison stared off into space as Julie sorted out her thoughts. None of this seemed to have anything to do with the baby her father was trying to give away. Now, even that seemed insignificant.

"Then I came back," he continued. "I had a couple hundred dollars for two years' work and a lot of ugly memories. The farmers who weren't drafted had done very well and I thought I could at least get my old job back. Ha! They told me that when I left, they had to hire a replacement and that they couldn't get rid of him now and they didn't need anybody else and they wished me luck. Luck! I used that up just by returning home in one piece!"

"Maybe I should have just let you stay with your aunt. Everybody said a father couldn't bring up a daughter all by himself. I suppose I was just stubborn enough to try to prove them wrong. I was convinced that you needed me but, looking back on it, I was the one who needed you. You were the one thing that kept me going. I suppose it was selfish of me, but I used what money I had to buy that medicine show wagon. I really did enjoy those years roaming around the country. Every time I fleeced one of those farmers, I enjoyed it immensely! But don't go bad-mouthing those lighting rods to me. How do you know they don't work? I might have saved a couple hundred farm houses. At least, I thought that was what I was doing."

"Alright, so maybe it was a bad way to bring up a daughter, but at least you weren't like all the other girls who never saw beyond their own horizon and who never met anyone but the boy next door."

Again there was a deep silence. Both were embarrassed about finally uttering sentiments that had been implied or ignored the last seven years. Finally in a weak voice, Julie said, "But Daddy, sometimes the most important thing for a kid is to be just like everybody else."

The simplicity of the statement hit Morrison with more force than anything he had experienced in the Great War. Nothing could have more clearly announced the end of his "Me and Juliette Against the World" existence. She was grown up, the future was her own, and there was nothing he could do about it. It would be their last trip together.

Morrison abruptly stood up, strode near the door and said, "Very well. I've been thinking about getting into something more permanent anyway. After tomorrow night, I'll return the films if I can. I'll find a job in Fargo or maybe the Cities. If I'm going to be a successful businessman, I may as well start acting like one. I will conduct myself in a manner that won't shame you in the eyes of anyone you may take a shine to. If they respect me, I will respect them. We can leave Vingelen with our dignity and their money. Will that suit you?"

Julie rushed to her father and put her arms around him. Morrison stiffened but Julie went on, "Please, Daddy. I didn't mean to hurt your feelings. I do love you and I will always treasure the life we have had together. I didn't always want to be like everyone else; I was proud not to be! But sometimes, well sometimes, I just wanted to be ordinary."

Morrison put his hands on her shoulders and said forcefully, "Don't say that. You'll never be ordinary. That's one of the reasons I don't want you to marry an ordinary farmer."

"Karl isn't ordinary."

"Well, if he is that special, I expect a little thing like last night won't put him off. If you don't see him again, then you'll know that he was as ordinary as the rest of the Scandinavian hayseeds around here."

As Morrison with his funny little strut magically restored went to the door, Julie said, "You still haven't told me about the baby."

This time her father's eyes actually twinkled as he said, "You leave that to me. A guy's got to have some fun, don't he?"

For several minutes Julie stared at the door that had closed behind her father. She knew that some day--perhaps some day soon--she would leave him, but she also knew that she would never abandon him. She had always known that she loved him, and now she was beginning to realize why.

10

Out Shocking

10

Saturday was a long, hot, nasty day. Karl and Paul spent most of it shocking for Arvid Bengston. They hated shocking. Everybody hated shocking. It was a tedious job following behind a grain binder picking up heavy bundles of grain and piling them in upright shocks. Half the time the tying mechanism wouldn't work and the twine would come undone just as a bundle was picked up. Then they had to make a knot in the twine and, if this was not possible, had to twist straw around the bundle and hope it held together long enough to be pitched into the threshing machine. Karl seemed to be mad at everything, even the grasshoppers perched on his beat-up straw hat which he had again filled with green leaves. Mrs. Bengston brought out a fine lunch, but Karl hated it and gave most of it to Paul. This act of kindness encouraged Paul to attempt conversation as they sat in the limited shade of the wagon.

"I don't mean to be nosy Karl, but are you planning to go into town tonight?"

"What for?" Karl snarled. "She probably left town as quickly as she could. I would have!"

Paul shrugged and said, "Maybe she'll stick around to see you. 'Ya ever think of that?"

Karl, suddenly optimistic again, said; "Geez, 'ya think she'd do that?"

"Well I wouldn't if I were her," Paul assured him, "but you never know. I thought I'd go into town tonight with the folks. I think they are planning to go to the movie."

"No! For God's sake, didn't you tell them about it?"

"Sure. But they never get a chance to see movies, and even though it doesn't make any sense to anyone, Ma sees it as her big chance. She was just tickled to death that it had been held over until tonight so she would have a chance to go. Pa doesn't want to go much. He keeps referring to that stupid baby. Hey, who do you suppose Morrison got to take care of the baby while he was running the show?"

Karl could not keep the disgust out of his voice. "You don't really think he has a baby to give away, do you? After what we saw last night? You're as gullible as all the other Norwegians."

"Well, he said he was going to give away a baby, didn't he? It's on all the posters. How's he going to weasel out of that?"

"Believe me, Paul, he'll find away." With that, Karl got up, put on his tough leather gloves, and proceeded to do the sloppiest shocking job of his life.

On the way back from the field Paul, in mock innocence inquired, "You sure you don't want to go along tonight? Everybody goes into town on Saturday night!"

"I can't think of anything I want to do less than sit in the Castle Garden Inn and talk to a bunch of farmers about the weather and the crops. 'Duh 'ya tink it's gonna rain? Well, it'll be a long dry spell if it don't.' Then everybody just sits around and grunts and farts until it's time to go home. I just can't take it."

"Hey, you're the one that wants to be a farmer, not me. You're supposed to love all that farmer shit."

"No offense, Paul, but you are more mentally suited for that than I am."

"Thanks a lot!"

"No, really, I mean it. It never seems to bother you to sit around and talk about absolutely nothing. Farming doesn't have to be uninvolved with intelligence. Things are happening other places. Why not around here?"

"I don't know, Karl. Why not around here?"

"Because we haven't evolved, that's why. And we haven't evolved because we haven't had to. Look who settled this country. The people who were too poor and too dumb to make it in

Scandihoovia, that's who. They came over and found land richer than they had ever dreamed about. They really weren't in much danger. Nobody was scared of the Indians by then. Heck, they didn't even have to clear trees or pick rocks! They just started plowing, seeding, and harvesting and for fifty years they have been plowing, seeding, and harvesting. Nobody has ever thought of anything else because nobody has ever had to. If it is a wet year or a dry year or one with grasshoppers, everybody moans. There's nothing anyone can do about that. Prices for our crops go so low you can't make a living and we do the same thing. We moan about it and then go out and vote for the same bunch of a-holes that we put in in the first place."

Paul sensed that it was time for one of Karl's soapbox orations. "So what should we do about it?"

"Get involved! We all gotta get involved! We gotta think. We gotta read, neither of which we do enough of now. It's been two years since the McNary-Haugen bill was introduced in Congress. What has happened? Nothing!

"Now look at George Peek," Karl continued. "He analyzed the situation and came up with an idea. He isn't even a farmer--he works for Moline--but at least he is smart enough to know that if the farmers don't have any money, he won't be able to sell them any plows. Senator McNary and Representative Haugen are smart enough to know something that will help the farmer. They get a good bill together in Washington. Does it pass? Are we farmers clever enough to use the economic power we have in this country to get it passed? Hell no! Even if it did pass, Coolidge would probably veto it and you know what half of the farmers in Vingelen would do? They would say, "Vell, da President, he must know vhat he's doing and ve've always been Republicans so I 'spose ve'll give him annudder chance.'"

Paul noticed another definite sign that Karl was getting worked up: "heck" had turned to "hell." Holding up his side of the conversation, Paul said, "So you think McNary-Haugen is the answer, huh?"

"Ya darn right. Look! The Agricultural Department figures out the ratio and price on each farm product using prices from before the Great War as a base. The government buys grain at that price, and sells it on the world market for whatever it can get. Here is the beauty of the thing: you charge the farmers an equalization fee based on the bushels they sell. It's fair. The big farmer pays his fair share, and the small farmer pays his fair share. Even Coolidge's Secretary of Agriculture is for it."

"Well, you don't have to convince me, Karl," protested Paul, "but I heard some guys in town the other night talking about how it was sort of socialistic."

"There you go, Paul. That's a good reason for not going to town and listening to those nincompoops. Mind you, I'm still not convinced that a little socialism might not be a good thing. Of course, you can't even get by with suggesting that anymore. It isn't socialism. If anything, it is creative capitalism. Hell, it will save the system. The most dangerous thing about a bill like this is that it just might cause some of these Norwegian farmers to think. If that happens, who knows what their future will be? And the Republicans sure don't want them to start thinking, because if they do, they will never vote for a Republican!"

Paul, who was actually capable of getting alarmed at Karl's radicalism, warned, "You better look out or they'll fry you like they're going to do with that Sacco Vanzetti or whatever his name is."

"It's Sacco and Vanzetti, and they aren't gonna fry."

"Wanna bet?"

"Ya! Er no, I guess not," said Karl, sadly. "The way things are going, they probably will."

"Maybe you ought to go into politics, Karl. You're too smart to be a farmer."

They had just reached the edge of the grove that surrounded the house. Ma was on her way to the barn to begin the milking. The cows, with their built-in sense of time, had gathered near the barn door. Karl and Paul walked on a few more yards before Karl said seriously, "Don't say that, Paul."

"Say what?"

"That I'm too smart to be a farmer."

"Why not? It's true. You ought to be going to college."

"You think I wouldn't like to go to college? I'd love to do that more than anything else in the world, but I can't and there's no use daydreaming about it. I used to think I'd like to go to college and become a professor, but you know what? If I went to college now, I'd go to become a better farmer. They got courses over at the A.C. in Fargo you wouldn't believe."

"Bullshit! If you went to college, you'd never go back to farming."

"Bullshit, yourself! What do you know about it? To you, all this place has ever been is a place to leave. But look at it. That corn is the prettiest green in the world. That wheat up on the hill is golden--not just yellow or tan--but golden. And look at the trees around here!"

"What about 'em?" demanded Paul.

"Except for those trees over by the lake, every tree that you see has been planted by someone, someone who loved this land enough to make it pretty, to make it like the home they knew back in the old country. This is our land, Paul! This dirt is gorgeous!"

"Weren't you just telling me that the settlers never did anything but mindless farming? Now you're praising them for beautifying the prairie."

"*Ja*, well, I take that back. The first generation pioneers were fantastic. It's the second generation that let their brains become degenerate organisms."

"Degenerate organisms? Now I know you should go to college."

"No, I've got a feeling I never will. I'll farm with Pa for a few years and maybe, like you say, I'll marry some local Norwegian's daughter and raise kids who are just as ordinary as everyone else's around here. I'll only be a farmer, but that doesn't mean I have to stop thinking. We got a lot of smart people in our community and others around here who have gone to college. Some have even become ministers, but many go away. They see their farms as places to get away from. Most of the ones who stay become consumed by such issues as who has the smartest dog. I gotta stay here because I have no choice economically, and because I love it too much to leave. Maybe you can't understand that but I hope that one day I find someone who will."

As they approached the house Karl said, "See what you can find out about Julie tonight, will you?"

Paul, who was sometimes awed and even envious of the passionate commitment Karl possessed, nodded.

That night Karl read a book about the aftermath of the American Civil War. He was reading about the carpetbaggers in the South and very consciously making comparisons with a certain movie entrepreneur in Vingelen. In the still summer night he could hear the sound of a Model T engine and he knew that Pa and Ma were on their way home. He was nervous just waiting to hear their report.

While Pa returned the empty cream cans to the cooler, Paul helped Ma take in the groceries. As she removed the groceries from a cardboard box, Ma said, "I don't know how that Nelson can get by with charging the kind of prices that he does at the store. Look at this! We got only two boxes of groceries and he wants over five dollars. Before the war we would have carried five boxes for five dollars worth of groceries. All he has to do is sit back and sell it to us. Maybe we should shop somewhere else. Pa keeps telling me it's a fine place to shop. Sure, I say, it's a great place to shop, but a bad place to buy!"

"You go to the movie, Ma?" asked Karl, apprehensively.

"*Ja*, sure."

"So, how did you like it?"

"Well, I guess it was pretty good," Ma reluctantly admitted. "There were a lot of different stories. But you know, I think I would rather have had just one story than all of those different ones. And I can't help wondering what happened to that Dawson Dick. 'Course I know it's only a story, but it looked like such a good one. But did you see those alligators? They kept opening their mouths just like you did as a baby. And them flamingos! I don't see how they can stand on them skinny little legs. But I couldn't figger out what was going on in that last reel, with all those guys with swords."

Karl looked over at Paul who grinned, shrugged his shoulders, and nodded.

"Well how did Pa like it?"

At this point Pa came into the house. "The guy ought to be locked up! We sit trew da dumbest movies I ever seen and den he has da nerve to come out and say dat dere veren't enough people dere to give avay a baby. *Fa'n i helvete!* Dere vere a lot of people dere. The place vas over half full, and dat's a big place. Dere musta been a hunert people dere. But no! He says dat dere ain't enough people who have paid to see his movies and so he says dat he vill be showing the films one more night yust to give people a chance and dat he vill have to give da baby avay tomorrow night! Who da hell would fall for dat and go into town tomorrow night, tew?"

Paul and Karl looked at each other. They both knew they would be in town tomorrow night.

11

Going to Church

11

It was Sunday morning. Karl had gone to church mostly to please Ma. It was the third Sunday of the month and that meant that the services were in Swedish. Karl had no trouble following the sermon. After all, he had been confirmed in Swedish and had memorized long sections of **Luther's Small Catechism** in Swedish. When he was a kid he always went to the two-week session of Bible school and it was entirely conducted in Swedish. Pastor Lindstrom always seemed to get more worked up preaching in Swedish than he did in English.

Pastor Lindstrom would never see sixty again. He received his theological training in Sweden and emigrated at the age of twenty-five because there were already too many Lutheran ministers in Sweden. It seemed only fitting that he should preach in the New Småland Lutheran Church (Augustana Synod) of rural Vingelen. Grey-haired and perpetually dressed in the somber black of his somber profession, he projected a masterful, somewhat scary, image.

When preaching in Swedish, he could dish out fire and brimstone with the best of them, but when he tried speaking in English--which he had to do two Sundays each month--the result was less impressive. He would sometimes be too literal. Whereas the Swedish "*Herre Gud*" sounded just fine, Pastor Lindstrom never grasped that in English "Mister God" sounded ludicrous.

There was always a chance that he would come up with a real gem such as when he proclaimed to the congregation that "the Lutheran pastors were the Reverse of Sin." It was not the pompos-

117

ity of the claim that delighted the parishioners, but the way in which he always managed to mangle English pronunciation. The Swedish dialect in Vingelen had mixed so much with the local Norwegian dialect that this, combined with the Pastor's unique pronunciation, resulted in the unfortunate fact that most of the congregation heard him say "the rev holes of sin" implying that Lutheran pastors were the ass-holes of sin. Karl grinned every time he thought of it.

New Småland Lutheran Church was a simple country church with a single high steeple. Not many in the congregation were very proud of it, especially when they compared it to the large church that had recently been built in Orebro. Yet, its green roof and white-sided walls made it one of the most picturesque churches in Western Minnesota. The country church was already forty years old and surrounded by a cemetery filled with weathered stones written in Swedish recording the births and deaths of pioneers already forgotten. The inside was simply furnished with practical and well-worn individual seats. At the east end was a simple white altar rail covered in deep red velvet, and on one side was a magnificent, carved pulpit. The altar was plain and adorned with two candle holders, each holding three candles. Behind the altar was a picture of Christ ascending into heaven. Every Sunday of every year, from childhood to dotage, the members of the New Småland congregation stared at that picture. To a large extent, it eventually formed their private theologies.

Opposite the pulpit was a small pump organ. Every Sunday for the last twenty-three years Mrs. Nordstrom had sat there pumping and sweating and looking as though she had been transposed into the world of the Godly. Those in the congregation over fifty worshiped her. Those between thirty and fifty gave her a measure of deep respect, and those under thirty made fun of her. She only had one speed for hymns be they for weddings or funerals, Christmas or Easter. Paul always professed to look forward to her Christmas selections, especially the *Joy to the World* dirge.

Today she was sweating more than usual. There was little one could do to escape the summer heat except to open the windows and the door. This, naturally, tended to distract the listeners.

Little Eddie Wahlstrom had been acting up and his mother had taken him outside where, right under the windows, she was threatening him with a spanking as soon as they got home. John Olson, whose farm was close to the church but who never attended, could be heard cussing at his dog for chasing cows.

Karl's mind wandered. Since Pastor Lindstrom was preaching in Swedish, there was no chance he would repeat Karl's favorite English phrase about the "gan-nashing and gan-nawing of teeth." Besides, Karl had a lot on his mind. He gazed out the window and saw a striped gopher sitting on old Sten Hansson's grave. For a time he ruminated on the incredible faith that the pioneers who had built this church must have had, but soon he was smiling over the memory of when Paul had snared a gopher during Bible School recess and had put it up in the pulpit. Mostly, however, he thought about Julie, Doc Morrison, and the eleven-month-old baby.

Paul had asked about Julie when he had been in town the night before, but no one had seen her all day. To be sure, Karl could appreciate the fact that she would be embarrassed about the whole situation, but it was hardly her fault what her father had done. He just had to see her tonight!

Pastor Lindstrom was preaching on a text from **Romans**, the fifth chapter, but Karl only vaguely listened. He thought about silently praying that he would see Julie again and kiss her as he had done in Orebro, but he wasn't sure that was the kind of thing one prayed for. In any event, by the time he had a suitably vague prayer composed about how everything should come out happy-- along the lines of "thy will be done"--he lapsed into reverie about the church and his childhood once again. His eyes were fixed on the deep maroon fringe that hung from the top of the velvet-covered altar rail. He remembered the game children played while they were waiting for their mothers to finish what they were doing in the church kitchen. With all seriousness and great intent of purpose, the kids would lift every strand of fringe and fold it backward over the altar rail. When this was completed, they would madly brush it back with their fingers as rapidly as possible. This made it possible to begin the game again.

Karl never went up for communion without feeling the urge to play with the fringe. With a start he realized that the rest of the congregation was singing *"Children of the Heavenly Father"*, known to all as a "good Swedish hymn." Loudly, and from memory, Karl joined in:

> "Nestling bird nor star in heaven,
> Such a refuge e'er was given."

After church there was an uncomfortable amount of talk about the movie show in Vingelen. The men had gone outside and stood under the tall oaks that had been there long before the church was built. Pa, unfortunately, seemed to be leading the discussion about what ought to be done to safeguard the community against the likes of Morrison. Karl wandered away. From a distance Karl could always tell when Pa was about to swear to underline his point because he furtively looked around to see if the minister, ladies, or children were near. Cussing, after all, was a man's sport and it was simply unsporting to cuss loudly near the church.

Threshing dinners were good, but Sunday dinners were always the best because no one had to work afterwards and therefore, people could pleasantly gorge themselves. Ma understood this. Today she served up baked chicken, corn-on-the-cob, and something called *slumgullion*. *Slumgullion* was spelled, pronounced, and made in a multitude of ways. Ma made it with new potatoes (the little ones that are eaten before the rest are ready), fresh peas, carrots and onions all mixed up in a cream sauce. The correct way of eating it varied. One could either eat the vegetables in large bites with a spoon, or mash everything up and use a fork. However it was done, the dish was consumed with inordinate amounts of butter and salt. Paul loved it, and proclaimed that he could be happy with *slumgullion* alone.

Karl liked it too, but he was more of a corn-on-the-cob lover. The best corn-on-the-cob in the world was grown in Minnesota, and Karl was loyal to it. He had felt a duty to be loyal to it for the last fifteen years. When he was eight years old, Ma, upon learning that Mrs. Lindstrom would be away for a week, had asked Pastor Lindstrom to Sunday dinner. Except for her confirmation, wedding, and possibly the births of her two children, this was the biggest day of her life. She would never serve anything as undignified as corn-on-the-cob for the minister especially since Paul had lost his front teeth and would eat the corn with the side of his mouth while butter, salt, and bits of corn cascaded down in the general direction of his plate. Karl deemed corn-on-the-cob, which he considered God's greatest gift, the only thing suitable to serve the pastor. Upon discovering it was not on the menu, he cried and wailed and obstinately marched out to the field to pick some himself. Called to the table, he produced the corn and demanded that it be prepared on the spot. It wasn't even sweet corn, but the field corn that Pa grew to feed hogs. Ma had been mortified and took Karl aside to point out that he would get a spanking the moment the pastor went home. She did not forget to follow through.

The whole episode had become part of family lore and Pa seemed duty-bound to remind Karl of this every time corn-on-the-cob was served. Nevertheless, Karl persisted in his appreciation of corn and now supervised its planting every spring. Carefully organized rows were planted at different times so that the corn would ripen over a broad spectrum of the season. Karl was proud of his corn-growing expertise.

Today's dinner was leisurely and filling. Karl was able to steer the conversation away from the movies, the baby, and Morrison by surpassing Paul's talents for talking about the crops and the weather. The oven had been on to bake the chicken and a nice apple pie, and this made the house terribly hot. Even so, one had to have a couple cups of coffee to make the dinner just right.

The rest of the day passed unbelievably slowly. Pa and Paul went to the lake to do some fishing. Karl had never enjoyed fishing. He didn't even enjoy eating fish very much. As they left, Karl employed his only fishing joke which he used every time Paul went fishing, saying "Fishing is nothing more than an exercise involving a pole with a worm at each end." Paul dutifully smiled and protested that Karl didn't know what he was missing.

Pa didn't have many scruples about working on Sunday, especially Karl's working on Sunday. He suggested that Karl do a little fencing. It was terribly hot and after replacing a couple of fence posts and tightening the wire a little bit, Karl gave it up and went behind the house to read a book and to dread the evening chores.

Karl was reading *Lord Jim*. As stories of the sea fascinated him, he loved Joseph Conrad. Karl had never seen the ocean, but he had been to Duluth and Lake Superior had been awesome that day. Conrad's vivid descriptions, and Karl's powerful imagination, brought the tale to life. Karl couldn't help wondering what he would do if faced with the decision which confronted Conrad's captain. Would he jump? Would he face his ultimate moment of truth and make the right choice?

With a certain degree of self-loathing he looked around him. The colors were all there. A red barn, red grainery, and red chicken coop. A white house with some hollyhocks and zinnias growing along side it. Some green trees and some green corn fields. Some gold and tan fields of already harvested grain. Karl thought to himself, there's no deep blue of the sea, no whitecaps, no limitless horizon. My horizon is confined by other people's red barns. What would have happened if Julie's old man was a decent sort, a settled resident of Vingelen who ran a store or something? As far as any future with Julie, it wouldn't make a bit of difference. I'd still be a twenty-three-year old living with my parents with absolutely nothing to offer her. I could always wait until Paul leaves, marry her, and bring her back to share my old room. Oldest sons did that kind of thing all the time back in Norway and Sweden. Or, I could marry her and strike off on my own for Detroit or someplace and get a job making cars. 'Course, I wouldn't have to go all the way to Michigan. I could probably get a job in Fargo or someplace. But the end result is the same--I'd have to leave here, and darn it all--I don't want to leave here.

Meanwhile, I do nothing. Sooner or later something is going to happen, but I can't just wait for it to happen. Things just don't work that way. I need to be up on the ship, leaning over the rail like Lord Jim and have someone yell at me to jump. That way, whether I jumped or not, I'd be making a decision. I'd somehow be in control of my life. I hate this kind of drifting, of taking things as they come. Paul is good at it. He can face the dumbest

Republican and remain apolitical. I can't even take one seriously when he complains about something. Sure as God made little green apples, something always comes along for Paul. I bet he'll have his own garage by the time he's twenty-five. The way that business is going, by 1935 he'll be a rich man. Well, good for him. By that time, maybe he can sell me my first used car.

Karl sighed audibly and picked up *Lord Jim* once again. Well, Jim, you shouldn't have jumped, but at least you did something, he thought. For the next two hours, Karl lived someone else's adventure.

12

The Assault

12

When chores and supper had each been completed with the same sense of duty, Karl and Paul were ready to go to town. A few people had questioned the propriety of showing movies on a Sunday night, but since the baby question was now occupying everybody's thoughts, this was no longer an issue. As they rode along, Paul looked forward to the evening with undisguised glee. Karl felt a sense of impending doom.

Paul was trying to cheer him up. "Everybody's going to be there, you know. I was talking to the guys last night and if this baby business turns out to be one of Morrison's swindles, it will be the last one he ever pulls in Vingelen. Reidar said he had seen a whole crate of rotten eggs behind the hatchery and said he could swipe them if we need them. *Ja*, I think tonight could be real fun."

"Ah, geez, Paul. You don't wanna do that. How's Julie gonna feel if I have to tell her that my brother has been pelting her old man with rotten eggs?"

"So, who's gonna know?" demanded Paul, cleaning his glasses while blindly driving with his elbows. "It'll be dark by the time the movies are over. If something is phony about the grand prize, Morrison deserves whatever we give him!"

"Well, count me out. I don't want anything to do with it!" Karl replied.

"By the way, I heard another good story about Morrison," added Paul. His voice made the information as tempting as possible.

"Oh, no. All right, now what did he do?" asked Karl, divided between loyalty to Julie and his own curiosity.

"Sigurd Nelson heard it from his uncle who knew some guy out in North Dakota. It seems that about the same time he was running that medicine show, he would buy eyeglasses from Woolworth's in Fargo. He went around to the farms west of Grand Forks passing himself off as an eye doctor. That's how come they call him Doc. Anyhow, he'd give these farmers a phony eye test and then sell them these dime store glasses for about a three hundred percent profit. One time he ran into a guy with eyes like a bat. The guy had glasses that were even cheaper than those Morrison was selling. The old guy told him, 'You ain't fooling me with them things. They don't make a feller see better.' Well, Doc Morrison says to him, 'You're right. You got me there. Actually the glass in here is just fake. That's how we make our money. What really makes you see better are the frames. See how they come down and pinch on both sides of your nose? Well, that's the whole secret. That's where the cryptic nerve runs. These frames ride on the cryptic nerve and stimulate your eyesight. Gosh you're a sharpie! No one ever caught me on this before. I tell you what I'll do. I'll just take the glass out and sell you the frames for half price. I'll lose a little money, but you gotta promise you won't tell anybody about this or I'll be out of business.' Well, sure enough, the guy buys 'em and now he thinks he can see like an eagle. You sure you don't want to throw a few eggs?"

"I gotta admit, it's tempting. But give him the benefit of a doubt. See how he gets out of this baby thing."

It was still twenty minutes before the show was to start. Paul parked the Model T near the hotel and Karl told him he would see him later. Karl nervously went into the hotel and asked for Julie. Fat old Arne Nygard was hunting flies with a brand new wire mesh flyswatter. In response to Karl's timid question he boomed, "Dat Morrison girl? Ya, she's still here. Yust saw her come in. You yust go up and knock on da door of room number 4."

As Arne smirked, Karl self-consciously went up the stairs and knocked on Julie's door. A scary thought struck him: what will I say if her old man's there?

"Who is it?" Julie asked, in a quiet but nervous voice.

"Ah, uh, it's me, Karl. I just wanted to see you and see if you were all right. I couldn't find you after you left the other night."

"I'll be right out."

True to her word, Julie was right out. They went down to the lobby and Arne managed to find something to do on the porch so they had some privacy. In spite of all her troubles, Julie looked wonderful. She was wearing what looked to be a new flapper dress and had a little hat on her head that allowed her bobbed hair to turn under at the most appealing angle.

"Gee, you look swell," Karl said. (Stupidly, he thought.)

"Well, this is my traveling outfit," said Julie, with a dismal sigh. "I got a feeling I'm going to need it. I still haven't a clue as to what my father is going to do, but I know one thing. I certainly haven't seen any babies around here." Julie seemed about to lose her composure.

"I'm sorry about the other night," she continued. "I just couldn't face you after that disaster in the theater. There you sat while everybody else was either laughing or getting mad. I felt everybody except you were making fun of me. Your friends were snickering about you because you were with me. I just couldn't stand it any longer. I had to get out of there." With this she started sobbing and burrowed her face into Karl's chest. Naturally he was concerned about the way she felt, but on the other hand, he was quite delighted to have her sobbing on him.

"There, there, there," he murmured, wondering why anyone would ever say, there, there, there. "Everything will be all right."

"How on earth can everything be all right?" she demanded.

Understandably, a long pause followed this question. Finally, Karl attempted to express the bright side.

"Maybe it's not as bad as you think. My folks went last night. My dad was disgusted, of course, but my mother actually seemed to enjoy the films. We don't get much in the way of entertainment here you know. At least it has given people something to talk about. Obviously your father is not going to give away a live baby, but maybe he has something else in mind. Maybe he's going to give away a doll and explain that, in the hands of a loving child, it will actually live. Or something... I dunno... Maybe he has something classy in mind and will give away a colt-- you know, a live baby horse."

"Do you really think so?" Julie sniffled.

"Sure!" Karl lied. "Let's go over there and see what happens."

"All right, if you're sure you won't be ashamed to be seen with me. But Karl? Will you sort of stay close to me and try to see that no harm comes to him? He is my father, and he has always been very good to me."

"Sure," said Karl, feeling protective and just a little heroic. "And I'll be very proud to be seen with you."

By the time they got to the Vingelen Theater most of the chairs were already taken. Karl and Julie walked among the grins and titters to take the last seats in the front row. By the time the movie started, people were standing all along the back wall.

The show itself offered no surprises. John Bunge, with a great deal of self-importance, threaded the first reel with the aplomb of one whose career decision had just been made. The audience sat enthralled with *Stagecoach to Deadwood*. So far, so good, thought Karl, but how are they going to react to *Gold of the Yukon*? Obviously, Julie was worried about the same thing, and when the Black Hills were replaced by the Chilkoot Pass nobody seemed overly upset. The mountains of California, where both movies had been filmed, were exactly the same, but that wasn't why the public accepted the switch. It appeared that most of the people in the audience already knew that the program would involve several reels of different movies. The Florida Everglades had never seemed more interesting, and everybody liked the Keystone Cops. There was some dismay at not being able to find out the fates of Black Bart or Dawson Dick, but everyone knew the real reason they were there. Who would get the baby?

At last, with a triumphant smile, John Bunge turned on the lights and thanked everybody for coming. Somebody yelled, "Let's give John a hand," and everybody did. Then all eyes turned to the front. There was Doc Morrison. It seemed as though he had been edging toward the back door, but Reidar Simonsen and Paul Thorson had moved their chairs in front of it. The silence was deafening.

130

Julie didn't dare look up. "What's he doing?" she whispered to Karl.

"Looks like he's going to make a speech," Karl observed.

"Oh no! That's what he does worst!"

"Ladies and Gentlemen," Morrison nervously intoned. "Attendance at this film has been such that I cannot afford to award the door prize previously indicated. If a community cannot support its cultural events at a sufficient level, I see no reason why it should be rewarded. Therefore, I regret to say, I will no longer be showing films in Vingelen."

The people in the theatre behaved much better than one would have expected. There were a few cries of "cheat," "crook," "liar," and "somebody should do something," but nobody did. To everyone's surprise, Morrison was allowed to walk out of the room unharmed. Few people noticed that Charlie Holm, Reidar Simonsen, and Paul Thorson had slipped from the theater.

Relieved at the reaction, Karl said to Julie, "I suppose you will be leaving soon. Do you know where you will be going? Are you going back to Orebro? I would like to see you whenever I can."

"I'd like to see you again too, Karl," she said, through an enchanting smile. "I think we might be living in Fargo for a while. Do you ever get to Fargo?"

"Not too often, but I just might be able to get there more often now," responded Karl through the teeth of a broad grin. "Uh, listen. You want to go over to the cafe for some coffee or something?"

"I'd really rather not. I mean, I'd love to go there with you, but after tonight I'd really like to avoid the people who were at the movie. I'm sure you understand. Let's just walk back to the hotel."

"All right," began Karl nervously. "As a matter of fact, I've got the car parked right by the hotel. Maybe you'd like to take a little drive. Uh, it's really lovely by the lake."

Julie agreed to this with an enthusiasm that made Karl's knee's tremble with anticipation. She took his arm and together they left the theater. The hotel was only about a hundred yards away and before they got half way there, it was obvious that something was happening. Both had to fight back the urge to run.

First Karl noticed a figure that looked like Reidar Simonsen standing on top of the hotel roof. His arm shot forward and Karl saw a white oval shape fly through the air and hit the back of the head of someone in a black suit who was running madly. On the porch he saw his own brother fling another object, and a third arm was raised behind a Model T parked in front of the hotel.

"My gosh! That's Daddy!" Julie screamed. "They're throwing eggs at him. He can't get into the hotel! Do something, oh please. Do something, Karl."

Sure enough, Doc Morrison was running as fast as he could down the middle of the street. At least five people were hurling eggs at him. As Julie watched in horror, her father stumbled and fell in the street. The eggs that had already struck him caused most of his suit to be covered with a caked dust. There was no doubt the eggs were rotten. Morrison, choking with threats and damnations, was now aiming for the safety of the Castle Garden Inn.

He didn't make it. From atop the Inn, letting fly with more ovoid ammunition, were Charlie Holm and Sigurd Nelson. Two others attacked from behind parked cars. More eggs flew from on top of the bank and from the side of the barber shop. The Vingelen vigilantes were striking back!

Karl was of the opinion that Morrison was getting exactly what he deserved but, in deference to Julie, he ran after him trying to stop a situation that was already clearly out of hand. He saw Paul duck behind the hardware store with a paper bag that obviously contained a supply of ammunition. He couldn't prevent Julie's old man from getting hit with eggs, but at least he could keep his own brother from doing it. As Paul lay in waiting, grinning and panting in anticipation of the target that was coming into range, Karl sneaked up behind him and grabbed the bag. Paul protested, but Karl was already turning the corner onto the Main Street. Morrison, looking rather shiny and yellow, was trying to make it to Flora's, his last possible refuge. Julie was running and crying, trying to catch up with him. At that moment, Rolf Norsen cocked his arm to deliver an egg at point-blank range.

132

Norsen was fairly new to the Vingelen community, but at the moment he seemed determined to fit in. Karl saw Julie coming out of the corner of his eye. It was his moment of truth. He was Lord Jim, and the men in the lifeboats were yelling at him to jump. He grabbed an egg out of Paul's bag and let it fly at Rolf.

There was a reason why Karl was never asked to join the Vingelen baseball team. As Julie watched in horror, Karl's egg missed Rolf by five feet and hit Morrison in the back of the head. Morrison lost his balance and stumbled into a telephone pole. The pole, being the more permanently established of the two, suffered the least. A trickle of blood oozed from an abrasion on Morrison's forehead, adding a touch of crimson to the grey dust and yellow yolk. Morrison literally crawled the last ten feet to Flora's door to claim sanctuary.

Julie cried, "Karl! How could you? I thought you were on my side. I never want to see you again!" She jerked her head around, stuck out her chin and, with tears running down her face, proudly walked into Flora's to be with her father.

All this had not gone unobserved. Johnny Bakken--slow of tongue, slow of foot, and slow of wit--was the town constable. He had moved his ample posterior from his favorite counter stool to watch, with undisguised appreciation, the events of the last ten minutes. Karl stood in a state of helpless shock as Johnny went by and muttered, "Nice shot." A feeling of hopelessness came over Karl as he slowly walked over to the Castle Garden Inn to drown his sorrows in a cup of coffee.

Meanwhile back at Flora's, Morrison had collapsed his smelly and slimy form into a chair. Julie helped him off with his coat and Flora kindly provided a bowl of water and a bar rag to wash off some of the rotten egg. There hadn't been many people in the cafe to begin with, and now it emptied rapidly of everyone except Julie, Morrison, Flora, and old Art Lein.

The new world had not treated Art very well. He never became fond of the English language, but became fond of American booze. He had a solid account with the local bootlegger and had conducted a major transaction with him earlier in the evening. Art's hair was white and his seemingly permanent stubble was white, but the whites of his watery eyes were red. He didn't have the slightest idea of what was happening.

Morrison loudly began to rave, "Where is the constable in this town? I need protection! I have my rights! Every one of those hoodlums should be jailed." At this moment, Johnny Bakken was about to enter Flora's.

Rolf Norsen, eager to be a part of things and feeling somewhat cheated that Karl's egg had done the job Rolf's egg was intended to do, came up with another idea. The Ku Klux Klan had experienced a tremendous revival in the 1920's. This anti-Negro, anti-Catholic, anti-Jew, anti-communist, anti-evolutionist, anti-birth control, and anti-intellectual organization had spread from the South into the North. By 1926 it contained perhaps five million members. The "Knights of the Invisible Empire" had recently called attention to themselves through a massive march down the middle of Pennsylvania Avenue in Washington, D.C. Even Fargo, which witnessed a black person only when the railroad porters happened to look out of the window, had a chapter. It was time, Norsen solemnly proclaimed, for the Vingelen chapter to form and activate itself.

Norsen found some excelsior in a packing crate behind the hardware store while Reidar Simonsen made a large cross from wood stolen from the lumberyard. The excelsior was wrapped around the cross and the whole thing was doused with gasoline siphoned from an Oakland sedan that some unlucky person had parked nearby. The lot across the street from Flora's was vacant, and the cross was erected in this place of prominence. Norsen struck a match. No one could doubt but that the Imperial Wizards and Grand Goblins were having a "Konclave" over the issue of the live baby fraud.

As the fiery cross burned on high, Morrison was panic-stricken. "I must call the sheriff," he screamed. "Only the sheriff can save me now! Where's the telephone?"

Flora, with the hint of a smirk on her face, dutifully showed him the wall telephone at the back of the cafe. Frantically spinning the crank, Morrison was soon in touch with Central. His first words were, "Call the Sheriff!" His second words were, "What's

134

the matter with the phone?" (Charlie Holm, standing along side the building with a pair of pliers in his hand, could have given the answer.) After a stunned silence Morrison gasped, "My God! They've cut the telephone wires."

The cross burned quickly. As soon as the excelsior burned off, the fire died. John Bakken slowly walked up and said, "All right, boys. Yew had yer fun. Beat it!" And, in fact, they had had fun. Nobody wanted to do any real harm to Morrison. The affair was over and there was nothing left to do but to talk about it over cokes and coffee and savor the moment. The group drifted over to the Castle Garden Inn to brag to all those who hadn't been part of it. Paul collected the morose Karl. Together they drove home with the mutual understanding that maybe they shouldn't tell Ma about it.

For the next hour, Morrison crouched in a booth in Flora's while Julie alternated between crying spasms and irate mutterings. At last John Bakken arrived. Morrison almost threw himself at his feet, imploring him for protection from the Klan. Bakken professed ignorance (which usually wasn't that difficult for him) about the whole matter. "I don't see no cross," he proclaimed truthfully. "Ve don't have no Klansmen in Vingelen. Why should anyone burn a cross here? Come on, I'll valk yew back to da hotel."

Under the constable's protection, Julie and Morrison emerged from Flora's. There was no one in the lot across the street. Most of the cars were gone from Main Street and only a couple of old men sat on the bench in front of the Castle Garden Inn. The three proceeded peacefully down the street and were soon safely in the hotel. For Julie and her father, it was a night they wished to forget.

135

13

The Investigation

13

Unfortunately, Morrison was not one to forget. He and Julie left town on the morning train without leaving a forwarding address at the hotel, but the station master of the Northern Pacific Depot reported to the people having morning coffee in the Castle Garden Inn that the Morrison's had bought tickets to Fargo.

To the residents of Vingelen this seemed to end the matter. But not to Morrison. After establishing Julie and himself in the home of his departed wife's sister, he crossed the river into Moorhead, Minnesota.

Moorhead was the county seat of Clay County and therefore was, to the rest of the county, sort of like what Paris was to the rest of France. Moorhead had been a railroad boom town in the preceding century and had held promise of becoming the titular capital of the Red River Valley. Land speculators, always looking for a quick buck, had managed to buy up a considerable portion of the town, and so there began a drift across the river to the little town of Fargo.

Minnesota taxes compared unfavorably to the taxes (or lack of them) in Dakota Territory. In time, Fargo became the center of commerce for the region. Still, Moorhead had prospered in its own right and, although it was only about one-half the size of Fargo, it boasted a population of about 10,000. Unlike other towns in the county which had all their businesses on one street, Moorhead had commerce on Main and Center Avenues with a few businesses and a railroad track in the middle. It had haberdasheries, tall grain elevators, broker's offices, a daily newspaper called appropriately **The Moorhead Daily News**, Woolworth's, a hospital, and more ex-taverns than a town its size could reasonably be expected to have.

Morrison, however, had not come to shop. He went directly to the Clay County Courthouse. Every one of Minnesota's counties had a courthouse which, more often than not, was the pride of the county. This was not the case in Clay County. The Clay County Courthouse was built during one of the leaner agricultural periods and had been erected without a keen eye to the future. Some called it charming, although it lacked both a recognizable architectural style and space. It did, however, have a gorgeous courtroom as Morrison would later observe. On this trip he searched for, and found, the door to the Sheriff's Office.

Morrison pushed past a man in the dark blue business suit and addressed himself to the uniformed man who was posting a notice on the bulletin board. "You the sheriff?" he asked.

"Nope," came the disinterested reply.

"Is the sheriff here?" Morrison demanded, straightening a hideous light green necktie.

"*Ja*," the deputy admitted.

"Can I see him?" asked Morrison, clearly annoyed at the deputy's laconic manner.

"I suppose so. Just turn around."

Morrison turned and eyed the well-dressed gentleman in the blue suit who had obviously been enjoying the introduction. He was only about thirty-two years old, and smooth of face and manner. No one could have guessed that this man was a county sheriff or that this man had, in fact, been re-elected to his second term as sheriff by a record margin. He walked forward and introduced himself.

"I'm Mel Johnson, Clay County Sheriff. What can I do for you?"

Morrison gave an odd little hop on his toes and squared his shoulders. "I'm here to lodge a complaint. Last night I was a victim of assault and battery in Vingelen. I do not know the names of the hoodlums except one, but I have a list of witnesses who can swear to what happened."

140

"All right. One thing at a time. Come, sit down, and we can write it up. Are you a resident of Vingelen, then?"

"Well, er, no. I just happened to be there on business," replied Morrison, as he nervously sat down beside the sheriff's huge wooden desk.

"So, what happened?"

Morrison straightened some sparse hairs over his bald spot and tried to jut out his weak chin. "I had just shown some films at the Vingelen Theater. As I was returning to my hotel, I was set upon by a number of young thugs who threw rotten eggs at me. I had done nothing at all to provoke them. It was a shameful and wanton attack upon my person. I tried to seek shelter in several places in the village but those hoodlums were everywhere. There must have been twenty or thirty of them. I finally reached safety in a cafe, but not before I had received a nasty blow to the head. It was only after we were in the restaurant that they revealed who they were. They burned a Ku Klux Klan cross on the other side of the street. When I attempted to call for legal protection, they had cut the telephone wires. It was only after several hours of the most vicious intimidation that we were able to make it back to our hotel under police escort."

"Police escort?" asked Sheriff Johnson in surprise. The only law official in Vingelen he could think of was Johnny Bakken, and it was ludicrous to think of him escorting anyone.

"Yes. Constable Bakken kindly guarded our passage to the hotel. I shudder to think what it would have been like had he not appeared. It is only too bad that he was not around earlier."

The sheriff nodded and suppressed a grin. Johnny Bakken had a reputation of leaving whenever trouble was near. He was sure Johnny had seen the whole episode with Morrison and was also sure that Johnny would deny any knowledge of it. Johnson decided to let it pass. Johnny needed all the praise he could get.

The sheriff continued, "And you can give no reason why they attacked you?"

"None whatsoever," Morrison indignantly replied. "They may have been upset because I did not award a door prize at my film showing, but it is certainly my prerogative to withhold a prize

141

if I do not consider conditions merit one. Given the attendance, I decided that no prize should be given."

"Can you identify any of your assailants?"

Morrison carefully studied his close-clipped fingernails and answered. "I saw many of them in the few days that I was in Vingelen, but I know the name of only one. I am ashamed to say that he has made the acquaintance of my daughter. His name is Karl Thorson."

Karl Thorson! thought Sheriff Johnson. I know him. That's that book-reading farmer I keep running into at the Moorhead Library during the winter. I can't conceive of him ever getting convicted for assault and battery. To Morrison he merely said, "And you know no other names of the 'twenty or thirty' of them that attacked you?"

"No. I hadn't been in town long and it was dark so I couldn't see all of them."

"All right," said the sheriff, wishing he had started his vacation a week early. "I'll get this written up and you can sign your complaint. I'll look into it this afternoon. I was going out to that part of the county anyway. Where can I get a hold of you?"

"I'm staying with relatives at 1129-1st Street North in Fargo. They do not have a telephone, but I shall call on you from time to time to check your progress in this matter."

"You do that," said Sheriff Johnson, somewhat ungratefully. "Just leave it to us and let us know if you think of any more names." With a feeling of satisfaction that he had done the right thing, Morrison returned to Fargo.

Sheriff Johnson was not unknown in Vingelen. He had carried the village in the last election. Furthermore, he was the only one likely to walk into the Castle Garden Inn in the middle of the week wearing a blue suit. The appearance of a sheriff, however well liked, always caused a certain amount of unease in a small town. Ironically, as the few people who were in the cafe watched him park his new Oakland and head for the Inn, none could think of anything that had happened in Vingelen the last few days that would have merited a visit from the sheriff.

It was early afternoon, and Mrs. Helgeson was the only person working in the cafe. Johnson approached her and asked if she had seen Johnny Bakken.

"Yonny? *Ja*, he's in the back room playing cards. I'll go back and get him for you."

"No, that's all right. I can go back there," said the Sheriff to the rapidly retreating back of Mrs. Helgeson. Although Johnson would not have cared one way or the other, she wanted to be sure the men got their nickels and dimes off the card table before the sheriff saw them. The Castle Garden Inn was not a casino! A short time later Johnny Bakken came out and sat on the stool next to the sheriff.

"How ya doin', Johnny?" asked the sheriff, as he grabbed Johnny's hand in his best electioneering grip.

"Oh, not too bad, I 'spose," admitted the constable. "Vhat brings yew all da vay out here?"

"What do you think?" asked Johnson, with a raise of his eyebrows. "I heard you had a little trouble in town the other night."

"Trouble in Vingelen?" gasped Johnny, for such things didn't happen without his knowledge. "Nei, I don't tink so. Who told yew dat?"

"A guy came into the office this morning by the name of Morrison. Says he was assaulted and that his life was threatened by the Ku Klux Klan. Know anything about that?"

Now Johnny was really perplexed. "Morrison? No, I don't know any Morrison. Say, dat vouldn't be da feller dat showed dose lousy movies last veek, vould it? A lot of people got real disgusted about dat. Guy like dat, he ought to be locked up."

"That may be, but nobody has filed charges against him. (Yet, thought the sheriff.) He, on the other hand, has filed charges against one of your Vingelen boys and claims that there were twenty or thirty others involved in assault and intimidation."

"Twenty or thirty! Haw! Dere veren't dat many. I doubt if dere vere even a dozen."

The sheriff immediately put a finger under the startled constable's nose. "Ah, so you do know something about it. Tell me what you know, Johnny. You're the law here and you must report it to the sheriff. That's the way it is."

"Vell, I really don't know much about it." Johnny was hesitating, trying to buy time to see if he had done something for which he could get into trouble. "I vasn't really around vhen most of da stuff happened, yew see. I had taken a valk over to da utter end of town up by da school, yew know, and by da time I got back dere vas nottin to see and I yust took dose people back to da hotel." Johnny's manner became more relaxed as the fib seemed solid and not too far from the truth.

The sheriff nodded. He was reasonably sure that Johnny was telling the truth and was only leaving out the singular fact that he had been on the spot when trouble started and after careful observation, had removed himself to the other end of town.

"But den I heard a few tings afterwards, yew know. It was nottin' serious. It vas yust some boys having some fun. Dat Morrison vas a real crook, I know dat. He didn't even give avay da baby."

"Baby! What baby?" Johnson demanded, thinking Bakken might not be the smartest law official in the state.

"Didn't he tell yew about da baby?" asked Johnny, in genuine astonishment.

"No. Suppose you tell me about the baby, Johnny," said the sheriff, leaning back on his stool with his back to the counter.

"Vell, dis guy, he puts up posters saying he's going to give avay a free eleven-month-old baby at da end of da picture shows. Nobody really believed him, of course, or at least most people didn't, but everybody vondered, yew know. Den he shows da pictures and he says not enough people came and so he vas not giving avay nottin'." At this point Johnny was thinking he needed some coffee and figured that the sheriff was in a good position to buy him some, and so he said, "Maybe ve should have some coffee."

The sheriff took the hint and held up two fingers in the air to Mrs. Helgeson. He paid and watched Johnny hold a lump of sugar with two fingers and dip it into the coffee and noisily suck the coffee out of it. After satisfying himself that Johnny was ready to resume his testimony, Sheriff Johnson asked, "Then what happened?"

"Vell, a few of da boys I guess, I mean, vat I heard, was dey

144

trew a few eggs at da guy. And da eggs, I guess, vas rotten. And dey chased him into Flora's Cafe and dat's vere I found him when I came around."

"Did anyone strike Morrison?"

"You mean hit him wit dere fists? Nei, dey yust trew eggs at him. Nobody did nottin' to hurt da man. Did he tell yew dat?"

"Well, he implied it. Tell me, who were the boys who threw the eggs at him?"

"Like I said, I vasn't around to see it actually happen. By da time I got back uptown, dere vas nobody around," responded Johnny, inwardly proud of his ability to protect his own.

"Morrison says he was forced to stay in the cafe for several hours while this gang terrorized him. Now Johnny, Vingelen isn't that big. Even if you made a 'tour of duty' around the school, you couldn't have been gone that long. You must have seen something," demanded the sheriff, leaning his face towards the constable.

Johnny, in response, leaned back and rather lamely admitted, "Vell, I saw some boys setting a little fire in da vacant lot dere, but it was dark, yew know. I couldn't really tell who dey vere. Besides, I didn't know it had anything to do wit dat guy dat dey were trowing eggs at."

"So you did see them throwing eggs," said Johnson, triumphantly.

"Well sure, dey was trowing eggs. Er, ah, dat's vhat I hear later, you know. And of course, by da time I get up to investigate dat fire, nobody's around and da fire is about out so I seen nobody dere."

"Yeah, that's what I thought, " nodded the sheriff. "Tell me, what do you know about Karl Thorson?"

"Karl Torson? Nottin' wrong wit Karl Torson. He's one of da best young guys around here. Vat do yew vant vit Karl?"

"Can you tell me where he lives?"

"Vell, you yust go about two miles east and den a mile sout' and den a mile east again and he lives wit' his dad, A.C. Torson. He's da feller who vorks in da elevator sometimes. Karl and his brother seem to do most of da farming out dere."

"Thanks. Ah, listen Johnny, if you hear of anyone who was involved in that Morrison business the other night let me know, will ya?"

"*Ja* sure, you bet. Tanks for da *kaffe*."

"Sure, Johnny. See you around."

Sheriff Johnson found the way out to the Thorson farm without any trouble. Ma was the only one home. Seeing a car with "Clay County Sheriff" painted on the side put her in a tizzy. The sheriff barely got the car turned off before Ma came running out of the house, asking in Norwegian if something had happened to her husband. The sheriff knew enough Norwegian to understand her question, but answered in English, "No, no, Mrs. Thorson. Everybody's fine as far as I know. I'd just like to have a word with Karl."

"With Karl? Has Karl done something wrong? Karl wouldn't do anything wrong. He's such a good boy. Are you sure you don't want to talk to Paul? Oh, look, there's Paul yust coming home now. Why don't you talk to him?" Ma, not used to talking to a sheriff, had by this time twisted her apron into a ball. Sheriff Johnson felt compelled to reassure her.

"Now, now. I'm sure everything will be all right. You just go back in the house and I'll have a word with your son."

Paul had just returned from the Hendrickson farm, the last of the farms in their threshing circle. The harvest was finally over for another year and Paul was feeling exceptionally lighthearted as he unhitched the team from the wagon. When he saw the sheriff approach, he was merely curious. In no way did he connect the sheriff's appearance with the events of the previous Saturday night.

Paul stood dumbly holding the horses as the sheriff walked up and said, "Hi. I'm Sheriff Johnson."

"Uh, ya, I know. Er, what can I do for you, sheriff?"

"Your brother around?"

"*Ja*. He's coming right behind me. Should be here anytime now. Anything I can help you with?"

"Well, I just wanted to talk to him about the business in Vingelen last Saturday night. I don't suppose you know anything about that, do you?"

146

Paul felt a sick feeling in the pit of his stomach. "Uh, what business is that sheriff?" he managed to ask, his mouth getting drier by the second.

"Seems some local boys terrorized somebody Saturday night and now he's filed a complaint for assault and battery."

"And you want to speak to Karl?" asked Paul, in disbelief.

"Yup," replied the sheriff, keeping expressionless eyes riveted on Paul. It worked. Paul blurted out. "He didn't have anything to do with that!"

"How come you're so sure he didn't?" Johnson quickly demanded.

Paul didn't quite know what to say. He was perfectly willing to clear Karl, but he wanted to know just how much the sheriff knew. He tried, quite transparently, to play it cagey. "I just know Karl. And besides, he was sort of sweet on Morrison's daughter so he wouldn't do anything like that."

"Did I say anything about Morrison? You seem to know quite a bit about this."

"Well, *ja*, I mean, everybody does, er, look, here comes Karl now," said Paul, abruptly turning his attention to a non-existent problem with the horse's reins.

Karl drove his team over to where Paul and the sheriff were standing. His first thoughts were that Paul must be in some kind of trouble. He hopped down off the wagon and manfully interposed himself between Paul and the sheriff and said; "Hello, Sheriff. What brings you all the way out here?"

"I won't beat around the bush on this Thorson. A guy called Morrison was in my office this morning and made some pretty serious charges. He's filed a formal complaint of assault and battery over an incident that took place in Vingelen last Sunday night and has named you as one of the perpetrators. He claims that there were a couple dozen hoodlums, but you were the only one whose name was known to him."

"Me! He accused me?" sputtered Karl.

"Yup. He claims you threw an egg at him which struck him in the back of the head, causing him to violently strike his head on a telephone pole. Did you do that?"

147

"No! Well, I mean, *ja*, I suppose I did, but it wasn't that way at all. I was trying to protect him."

"You were trying to protect him by throwing an egg at him? Doesn't sound particularly effective, does it?"

"I wasn't throwing at him. I was throwing at somebody else who was going to throw an egg at him."

"Oh yeah? Who was that?"

"Look, Sheriff," interrupted Paul, "he's telling the truth. Karl wasn't in on this at all. I'm the one you want, not Karl. He was doing everything he could to stop us."

"All right, now we're getting somewhere. Who's 'us'? Who else was there?"

"I'm not going to tell on the other guys. I'm sure you can find that out on your own, but Karl wasn't one of 'em."

"All right, boys. I'm beginning to get an idea of what happened here. You're right. I won't have any trouble finding out who else was in on this. In the meantime, I want you both to come to Vingelen tonight. For now, consider yourself both under arrest and don't bother trying to warn anyone else. Personally and privately, Morrison probably got just what he deserved. But as an officer of the law, I've got to see this thing through. Meet me in the Castle Garden Inn at eight o'clock tonight."

Karl and Paul stood helplessly by as they watched the sheriff get back into his Oakland and leave the farm. Paul expressed what they were both thinking, "*Nei Fa'n*! What are we going to tell Ma?"

When they got back to the house, Ma was silent and avoided their eyes. They knew that curiosity was eating away at her and Paul hoped that Karl, who was always so good at saying just the right thing to Ma, would tenderly explain the situation. When he pointedly remained silent, Paul knew it was up to him. "I suppose that you are wondering what that was all about, huh Ma?"

Ma was wonderful. She simply looked up at him and fearfully asked, "Are you in trouble, son?"

Paul told the whole story, taking pains to point out Karl's innocence. On the whole, Ma took it well with only a minimum of "tsk-tsks" and "for shames". When Pa got home, Paul went

148

through the whole story with him, although he related it with a little more humor and a little more pride. Pa was essentially delighted with the account, but was somewhat disturbed at the prospect that the boys might have to spend time in jail instead of getting the fall plowing done. All in all, the folks took it better than Paul thought he had a right to expect.

Meanwhile, the sheriff had gone back to town. There is something awfully threatening about a sheriff in a blue suit who can whip out a badge and show it to a twelve-year-old boy. Sheriff Johnson had spotted Palmer Lein shuffling down the street as he drove into town. He pulled his car right in front of him, jumped out, flashed his badge and said, "You're in big trouble, boy." Little Palmer was appropriately terrified so the sheriff had him in the palm of his hand.

"I understand that you were one of the guys who threw rotten eggs at Morrison last Sunday night."

Palmer stuttered out a desperate cry about not wanting to go to jail and proceeded to tell the whole story. He named Knut Andersson, Clarence Andersson, Charlie Holm, Reidar Simonsen, Rolf Norsen, Swen Sandquist, Sigurd Nelson, and Paul and Karl Thorson as being part of the attack on Morrison.

"Wait a minute," said the sheriff in his most threatening manner. "That's only nine. Who were the rest of them? Are you sure you weren't in on this? Who are you protecting?"

Palmer started to bawl and insisted that he had named everyone. After a few more threats, and after eliciting from young Palmer the promise that if he thought of anyone else he would inform "the law" immediately, the sheriff let him go. Palmer had probably never dashed away faster in his life.

Sheriff Johnson leisurely walked over to the cafe and got directions to the farms of the people named in Palmer Lien's testimony. The rest of the afternoon was filled with notifying those individuals that they were under arrest and demanding that they appear in Vingelen at eight o'clock that night. It was unfortunate, thought the sheriff, that the kid had named Karl Thorson. He would also have to be under arrest like everybody else, although the sheriff had by this time no doubt that his story was true. As it

149

turned out, the situation was even more unfortunate for Swen Sandquist. Although he regularly hung around with the rest of the guys, on that particular night he had not even been in town. He was, in fact, deeply sorry to have missed it. When Sheriff Johnson told him to consider himself under arrest for assault and battery against Morrison, Swen was actually grateful and promised to be in town along with everyone else.

Calling on Johnny Bakken again, Sheriff Johnson arranged for the theater to be opened up for a hearing. He ascertained that old Magnus Rian was still the acting justice of the peace for the village. That pleased him for Magnus was a clear-minded, old immigrant who could take his duties seriously or not, whatever the occasion warranted. At this point, the sheriff wanted a minimum of officialdom or officiousness.

The Castle Garden Inn was crowded that night. All those who had been officially charged were there, of course, but the news had spread and almost everyone who could get away was there to see what the sheriff would do. They were disappointed when Sheriff Johnson, Johnny Bakken, and Magnus Rian led the nine young men down the street and across the highway to the theater where only those with any business were allowed in. Even John Bunge, who argued that he should be admitted because he was the projectionist, was turned away. The sheriff motioned to the boys to take a seat. He moved a chair up front for Magnus Rian, and with Johnny Bakken leaning against the door, the sheriff was satisfied that nobody could get in. He addressed those present in his most official manner.

"You have all been charged with a most serious offense. Now I'm sure that most of you meant no real harm to Mr. Morrison last Saturday night, and I'm sure I'm right in thinking that most of you thought he could take it like a good sport. Well, he didn't. You may have thought that you were just teaching him a lesson and having a little fun. Again, he didn't think so. Now if it were up to me, I would just give you a warning, or at the most tell the justice of the peace here that you should each pay a small fine. But the fact of the matter is that you have been charged with a serious crime. I have no alternative but to honor this complaint and see to the due process of law. I have talked the matter over with Mr. Rian. He assures me that you are all local boys of relatively good reputation." (The sheriff looked over at Reidar Simonsen when he said the word "relatively.") Reidar was properly embarrassed, and for once had no wise crack.

"What I have suggested, and what Mr. Rian has agreed to, is to have you bound over on your own recognizance until such time when the case comes to trial. In the meantime, I will try my best to get Morrison to drop the charges, but I must tell you that I wouldn't be too hopeful that he will. The story that he told me doesn't resemble what I have heard here today, but I'm convinced that he believes his version. We're not going to ask you to post bail, but I want each of you to swear that you won't leave the state without informing my office and to swear to appear in Clay County Court on the day when this case comes to trial, if it ever does. In the meantime, don't act smart about this. If you are convicted of assault and battery, you could face a prison sentence. And don't, whatever you do, let me hear about any of you getting into trouble in the meantime. Do I make myself clear?"

Everyone nodded that things were indeed clear. One by one the young men who had been charged with assault with deadly rotten eggs gave their assurance to the justice of the peace that they would appear on any date so requested by the Clay County Court. With that, Magnus Rian dismissed them and they walked out of the theater to meet a crowd of curious people and to report on the proceedings. Most of the soon-to-be defendants drifted off to the Castle Garden Inn, but Karl stayed behind and walked with the sheriff back to his car.

"Uh, Sheriff. When Morrison came to your office this morning his daughter wasn't with him was she?"

Johnson sympathetically put his hand on Karl's shoulder and said, "Nope. Sorry about that. But if I do see her, I'll tell her that you asked about her."

Karl permitted a rueful grin to spread across his face and said, "*Ja*, do that."

14

The Uffda Trial

14

If one had bought a copy of the **New York Times** from a vendor on Wall Street on the morning of Wednesday, September 29, 1926, one would have gained a clear picture of the important trends and attitudes sweeping America in the middle of the Roaring '20s. The newspaper proclaimed that Al Smith had just won the Democratic nomination for the governorship of New York on a "frankly wet platform." There was more news about the Harding scandal as the Teapot Oil Lease was declared a fraud and Harry Sinclair and Albert Fall were denounced by an appeals court. A new and lasting land boom was expected in Miami even after its devastating hurricane. On the international front, the **Times** reported that "the French still balk at debt accord." Along the Great White Way, Lillian Gish was starring in the "*The Scarlet Letter*" in New York's Central Theater. Gene Tunney told how he had beat Jack Dempsey, and the sport pages observed that "Yankee pitching seems to have an edge on that of Cardinals for the approaching World Series." If one had bought a copy of the **Moorhead Daily News** along Center Avenue that day, the big news was "Vingelen Egg Case to Open Today."

The front page story continued:

"The trial of nine Vingelen area men on a charge of assault and battery begins today at the Clay County Courthouse. The men are accused of assaulting Mr. Henry Morrison, currently living in Fargo. Mr. Morrison has charged that on the night of August 29th he was assaulted by 'about two dozen' Vingelen men who caused him grave bodily harm and made undefined threats against his person.

"After extensive investigation of the incident, Mel Johnson, Clay County Sheriff, arrested Charlie Holm, Reidar Simonsen, Sigurd Nelson, Knut Andersson, Clarence Andersson, Rolf Norsen, Swen Sandquist, Paul Thorson and Karl Thorson– all of rural Vingelen– and released them on their own recognizance. The sheriff would give no answer when questioned about the other fifteen or so men believed to have taken part in the disturbance, but an unnamed deputy is reported to have said that 'Morrison was probably exaggerating about the total men involved.'

"The incident stemmed from a series of movies shown at Vingelen on the evenings of August 27th through August 29th. It seems that Morrison had promised to give a door prize of an eleven-month-old baby. However, after the final showing, when no such door prize was forthcoming, a number of young Vingelen men are reported to have pelted Morrison with rotten eggs. Morrison also claims that he was threatened by the Vingelen chapter of the Ku Klux Klan.

"The trial is expected to bring out information on two of the more puzzling aspects of this case: Where did Morrison intend to get an eleven-month-old baby, and how could he have given it away without breaking a number of state laws? The defense intends to examine this question very closely. The second major question involves the existence of the Ku Klux Klan in Vingelen. This reporter spoke to a leading Klan member of the Fargo chapter (who, understandably, wished to remain nameless). He implied that no one in the Fargo Klan had ever heard of even one Klan member from Vingelen. The Clay County prosecutor is expected to determine if a Klan 'conspiracy' existed in Vingelen.

"The trial is expected to begin at 10:00 a.m. before
District Judge Miles Lambert. A six-member jury will
be impaneled to hear evidence. State Senator Lester
Westgaard from the firm of Winston, Tenessen, and
Westgaard, will represent the defendants."

Karl and Paul had driven to Moorhead with Rolf Norsen and
Sigurd Nelson. Ma had seen to it that they were dressed in their
Sunday best and had delivered a practiced lecture on how they
should behave before the judge. Pa grunted that they "better be
home tomorrow to do some plowing", but then turned a little more
serious and shook their hands and wished them luck. Such an
overt display of affection from Pa was rare and it had a sobering
effect on the brothers. By the time they reached the courthouse,
however, they were in remarkably good spirits as they relived the
events of the evening that had brought them to this day. Karl had-
n't heard from Julie since the incident, and by now he was actually
glad that his egg had found the back of Morrison's head.

Five of the other defendants were already seated when Karl
walked into the courtroom. The gallery was packed with friends,
reporters, and the curious. At ten minutes after ten, the bailiff
commanded all to rise for the entrance of Judge Miles Lambert.
The judge was an imposing figure without his robes but attired for
the courtroom, he looked positively magnificent! He had steel
gray hair, penetrating blue eyes, and a face that looked incapable
of smiling. Reidar Simonsen audibly gasped when he saw him.

The selection of the jury was a short formality. Neither the
prosecution nor the defense seemed to have any concern as to the
suitability of the jurors for deciding such a case, and by 11:00
o'clock the trial was ready to begin. The judge made his opening
statement:

"Gentlemen of the jury. You have been called here
to decide the case of *The State versus Andersson,
Andersson, Holm, Norsen, Sandquist, Simonsen,
Nelson, Thorson, and Thorson*. The state charges that
on the night of the 29th of August last, the said defendants did willfully and with malice inflict grave bodily
harm on the person of Mr. James Morrison....huh?....oh,

157

excuse me...Mr. Henry Morrison in the Village of Vingelen in the State of Minnesota. And that furthermore, the defendants did willfully and with forethought threaten the bodily health, perhaps even the life, of the said, er, ah, Henry Morrison."

Turning at last to the boys from Vingelen, the judge proceeded, "You have each been charged with the serious crime of assault and battery. As I call out your respective names, I ask that you each rise and respond to the charges. Mr. Clarence Andersson, how do you plead?"

Clarence nervously stood and turned to Lester Westgaard, the defendants' attorney. "What do I say? What do I say?"

"Just say 'Not Guilty', sit down, and shut up. I'll take care of everything."

Clarence did as he was told and the other eight defendants, following his example, also stood when their names were called and replied simply, "Not Guilty." After some opening remarks by both the prosecution and the defense, "Doc" Morrison was called to the stand. With a supercilious upward tilt of the chin, he swore on a somewhat soiled black Bible to tell the truth. Urged to relate his version of the events of the night of August 29th, he turned appealingly to the judge and began, "You see, Your Honor, it was this way." One of the reporters from the *Fargo Forum* let out a hoot at this attempt to establish utter candor, but the judge merely said: "Will the witness please address his remarks to the jury?"

Rubbing his sweaty palms on his baggy gabardine pants, Morrison accordingly turned to the jury. The sight was not reassuring to him. A couple jurors were actually grinning, one was occupied with a crossword puzzle from the newspaper, and a fourth seemed to be dozing. These were the encouraging ones. The other two looked at him with unconcealed contempt. Undaunted, Morrison began his testimony anew.

"Gentlemen of the jury." (Another reporter guffawed.)

"On the evening of the 29th day of August, I was engaged in showing a series of films in the Vingelen Theater. Many people appreciated my attempt to bring some entertainment into such a small town and I solemnly swear that no one ever asked for their money back. If they had, I certainly would have refunded it cheer-fully."

Those people in the crowd from Vingelen began to buzz among themselves. It appeared that Morrison's statement, prepos-terous as it may have seemed, was probably true. Everyone had meekly submitted to Morrison's scam and had written it off as a lesson.

"In any event," Morrison continued, "following the comple-tion of my film series, I was on my way back to my lodgings when I was set upon by a large number of hoodlums who threw rotten eggs at me. Not only did the eggs cause pain when they struck, but they cost me a great deal of money for cleaning my clothes. I was pursued through the streets of Vingelen and finally fell when an egg struck me in the back of the head with such force that it lit-erally knocked me into a telephone post, causing a near concus-sion. By this time my daughter had joined me, and we were final-ly given refuge in a local cafe. The intimidation continued, how-ever. When we attempted to summon authorities, we discovered that someone had cut the telephone wires. These hooligans then showed their true colors by joining with other members of the Vingelen Ku Klux Klan and burning a cross in the field across the street from the cafe. Were it not for the kindly escort by Constable Bakken, we may never have arrived safely at our hotel."

At the mention of Johnny Bakken as an intrepid protector, most of the members of the gallery who were from Vingelen began to giggle. Judge Lambert had only to look in the general direction of the disturbance and an immediate silence followed.

The Clay County prosecutor seemed to find his job distasteful. Nevertheless, he asked Morrison, "And did you at any time do anything to cause this attack upon your person?"

Morrison indignantly replied, "No, sir, I did not!"

The prosecutor turned away and mumbled, "Your witness, Counselor." Judge Lambert intoned, "Does the defense wish to cross-examine?"

Lester Westgaard was a successful politician because he was a good showman. He took his time gathering up his papers before telling the judge that he did have a few minor points that he want-

159

ed to clear up with the witness. Westgaard was perhaps the only man in Clay County who dressed sharper than Sheriff Johnson and for this performance, before a group of people from the western part of the county whose votes would be needed in only five weeks, he was at his spiffiest.

After a dramatic pause and a superficial glance at his notes, Westgaard spun on his heel and dramatically confronted the seated Morrison. "In the posters advertising your '*film series*,' you promised that a live eleven-month-old baby would be given away. I have in my possession a copy of that poster which I should now like to place in evidence. Do you acknowledge that you put up, or caused to be put up, this poster?"

Morrison carefully examined the flimsy poster and muttered a terse, "Yes."

"I don't think the jury heard you, Mr. Morrison. Is this your poster?"

"Yes."

"Will you please inform the court about this so called door prize?" asked Westgaard with a sneer of disgust.

"It was a rooster," Morrison mumbled.

"What?" asked Westgaard, who was as surprised as everyone else at this testimony.

"It was a rooster," responded Morrison with an air of honest dignity. "I was going to award a baby rooster. I never said that I was going to give a live *human* baby away. That certainly would be against the law. You will notice that nowhere on that poster does it promise that the prize will be a live human-type baby."

"That appears to be true," allowed Westgaard, "However, on this particular poster, there is a picture of a live Negro baby prominently displayed above the words, 'Live eleven-month-old baby to be given away.' Don't you think that this poster therefore implies that the baby pictured will be the prize?"

"Certainly not. It merely implies that Negro children like to eat chicken."

Not even the stern look of Judge Lambert could control the members of the gallery at his point. While a minority of people were outraged by the implicit racism in Morrison's reasoning, most

160

roared with laughter. The judge himself was disgusted and banged his gavel to restore order.

"I would like to return to this point later, if I may," continued Westgaard when order had been restored, "but first I would like to ask you a few questions about the charge that the Ku Klux Klan exists in Vingelen and that it threatened grave bodily harm. Tell me, Mr. Morrison, what evidence did you see of the Klan?"

Morrison replied indignantly, "I have already testified that they burned a cross near the cafe where I had taken refuge. That certainly is evidence of Klan activity."

"Did anyone identify himself as a member of the Ku Klux Klan?"

"Well, no, not exactly."

"Did you hear any Klan slogans, songs, or direct threats?"

"Not in so many words, no, but the implication was there."

"Did you see anyone wearing sheets?"

"No, but it was dark outside."

"So the only evidence you can give the court of the existence of a Vingelen Ku Klux Klan conspiracy to do you bodily harm was the existence of a burning cross?"

Morrison reluctantly agreed that this was the extent of evidence of a Klan conspiracy.

"Did it ever occur to you that you may simply have been the victim of a prank?"

"After the way I had been treated? Pelted with rotten eggs?"

Westgaard, in a voice of Christian charity, countered, "Mr. Morrison, if they had really wanted to do you grave bodily harm they could have used rocks."

At this, the prosecutor's knee jerk reaction was to protest and voice an objection, but the logic in Westgaard's point was apparent. He felt silly enough prosecuting this case and was not about to jeopardize his promising legal career by arguing against such an obviously popular sentiment. Besides, from his brief conversation with Morrison, he had formed an instant disliking for the man. He would prosecute the case, but that didn't mean he had to try to win it. Westgaard dramatically let the point sink in and, with a wave of disdain, said, "No further questions at this time, Your Honor."

161

The next witness to be called was Art Lein. After all, Lein had been the only other customer in Flora's when the cross was burned. Flora herself pleaded that she couldn't leave the cafe for a whole day and had been excused from testifying once Art Lein's testimony was assured. Nothing would have been easier, of course, than for Flora to close the restaurant for a day. Few people went in there before supper time anyhow, but the last thing she wanted to do was testify for Morrison. Art Lein, on the other hand, could not have been more pleased. The people in the gallery from Vingelen were shocked to see him clean shaven, newly shorn, and wearing a relatively clean shirt. He placed his hand on the Bible and when asked if he swore to tell the truth, he answered unhesitatingly, "*Ja.*"

The prosecutor began, "Now Mr. Lein. Were you in Flora's Cafe on the night of August 29th, 1926, when Mr. Morrison and his daughter entered?"

Art was momentarily stunned. Nobody had called him Mr. Lein in years. At last Art became aware that the prosecutor was probably addressing him and he responded, "*Ja*, I vas dere."

"Could you tell us, in your own words, what you saw that night?"

"Vell, I really vasn't feeling too good at da time, yew know," (At this, most of the Vingelen crowd, who were well aware of Art's fondness for anything with alcoholic content, openly snickered,) "so I don't know vat time it vas. I guess I vas da only one dere in Flora's place. Everybody else had gone to da movies, yew know. Vell, I didn't vant to go to dem tings. So anyvays, I vas yust sittin' dere ven dis fellow, he comes tru da door followed by dis kind of purdy girl. I didn't know who he vas, but I tought dat maybe he had had a nip or two hisself, yew know, becuss he seemed to have a hard time standing up. Den I noticed dat he had a little blood on his forehead but dere vas also some slimy stuff all over him. And boy, let me tell yew, he yust stunk someting awful. So anyvays, here I vas trying to figger out vot vas going on, and he says someting about how I had to save him. *Er du gal?* (Are you crazy?) I asks him, but den I figger he don't speak no Norsk so I yust gave up on him and he didn't vant to talk to me no more den.

He vas asking vere da constable vas so I figgered he vas looking for Yonny Bakken, but den he got Flora to give him da phone. He didn't seem to be able to work it right for some reason and so he gave up dat and den he yust sat down for a while and Flora and da girl, dey got some vater and some rags and stuff and dey cleaned him up a little. Boy, did he need dat! He yust stunk someting fierce!"

Sensing that hearing the story in Art's own words was not the best strategy, the prosecutor decided it was wiser to put words into Art's mouth. "Now Mr. Lein," he soothingly continued, "would you say that Mr. Morrison was in obvious distress, discomfort, and anxiety?"

"No," replied Art.

"No?" gasped the prosecutor, "Why wouldn't you?"

"Cus I don't know vat dat means," replied honest Art.

"Well then, Mr. Lein, what did you think when you saw Mr. Morrison come into Flora's Cafe, bleeding and covered with eggs?"

"I yust tought '*uffda*!'"

"*Uffda*, Mr. Lein? *Uffda*? What do you mean?"

"I mean *uffda*!"

"What does *uffda* mean, Mr. Lein?"

"Vot does *uffda* mean? Don't yew know English, den? It yust means, *uffda*. Yew slip in da barn ven yew got yer Sunday pants on, dat's *uffda*! Yer flask gets a little hole in it, and dat's *uffda*! Yer daughter starts going out wit an Irish Catlik, dat's *uffda*! And by golly, ven I saw dat guy stagger into Flora's, dat vas really *uffda*! Vot more can I say?"

"Yes, Mr. Lein," said the prosecutor, obviously trying to hurry the testimony. "Now, can you tell us how long Mr. Morrison and his daughter were forced to stay in Flora's Cafe?"

"No, I don't tink so, " replied honest Art, who had just taken an oath.

"Well, then, can you make an estimation?"

"No, I don't tink so."

"Can you at least tell us approximately what time they left the cafe?"

163

"No, yew see, I tink I fell asleep a little bit dere. Flora, she voke me up about midnight, I suppose it vas, ven she vanted to close up, yew know."

The gallery roared, but the prosecutor wanted to make sure that his main point was made. "You can swear, however, that you did see Mr. Morrison covered with rotten eggs and that he had sustained a severe head injury?"

"Vell, I don't know how severe it vas, but he looked a little woosey, *ja*."

"Now, think about this carefully, Mr. Lein. What was the effect of the burning cross on Mr. Morrison? Did it provoke fear? Did Mr. Morrison have reason to think that his person was threatened? Did Mr. Morrison's daughter become frightened? Just describe what you observed when the cross was burned across the street from the cafe."

This time Art looked a little embarrassed. His blush made his red nose practically blend in with the rest of his face. He mumbled, "Nottin'."

"What did you say? I didn't catch that."

"I didn't see nottin'. I guess I must'a fell asleep before dat."

"But Mr. Lein," protested the prosecutor, "when Sheriff Johnson questioned you, he asked you if you were aware of the cross and at that time you replied that you were. Why do you now deny that you saw it?"

"Nobody asked me if I seen it. I never said I seen it. Da sheriff he yust asked me if I vas avare of it. Shit, da whole town vas avare of it da next day."

At this, the judge intervened reminding the witness to watch his language. Art misunderstood and apologized for talking *Norsk* \'nd promised to "talk American for da rest of da time." The prosecutor didn't know if he should be euphoric because his witness had proclaimed that the whole town knew about the cross, or if he should be depressed because his only on-the-scene witness had denied seeing it. Clearly the witness's own testimony was based on hearsay which would not be admissible, but at least it would now be hard to deny that a cross-burning had taken place. Given better circumstances, the young prosecutor thought, I could turn this trial into an impassioned plea for civil liberties and make a name for myself by attacking the Ku Klux Klan and everything it stands for. In this case, however, instincts tell me to ignore the whole thing. He rather abruptly said, "Thank you, Mr. Lein. I have no further questions."

All during this time Karl had searched the gallery for the one face that he cared about. Julie would have to be here, he thought. After all, she was an eyewitness to the whole thing. He had gone down row after row and carefully examined each face. Now, as the prosecutor finished his questioning of Art Lein, a large lady in the second row shifted her position, and suddenly there Julie was. For the rest of that morning's testimony Karl would continue to look at Julie, but Julie determinedly kept her face turned away from the area where Karl and the rest of the defendants sat. He heard very little of the defense attorney's cross-examination of Art Lein.

Lester Westgaard usually relished scenes like this. He could make old Art Lein say anything he wanted him to, but this was an election year. It would do his standing in the eastern part of the county no good to make a laughing stock out of one of its residents, no matter how ridiculous he may have been. He treated Art with almost exaggerated respect and sympathized with him each time Art made the spectators in the gallery nearly roll in the aisles, and the occasions were many. Art, it seemed, just could not understand how it had come to pass that he had fallen asleep, and Westgaard made no reference to the possibility that he may have been drinking. Westgaard had no difficulty in getting him to minimize the extent of Morrison's injuries, for he soon had Art referring to them as "a little bump on da head, dat's all." He also allowed Art to tell him no less than six times the extent to which Morrison stunk up the cafe. At the completion of the cross-examination, Judge Lambert was clearly disgusted, bored, and wanted his lunch. He adjourned the court until two p.m. and hastily retreated to his chambers. Everyone was in a good mood except the prosecutor, Morrison, and Karl.

As soon as the judge left the courtroom, Karl tried to get up to intercept Julie. This proved to be impossible. By the time he reached the corridor, she was nowhere to be seen. Meanwhile, Westgaard had called all of the defendants together for a little conference and Karl had to return to the courtroom.

"I'll just keep you a minute, boys, and then you can all go out and get some lunch. I want you back here by one-thirty. Now, I really haven't had a chance to talk to all of you about what you did, and I gotta admit that it is a little unusual for you all to be tried together like this. Lambert, however, didn't want to waste any more time and wouldn't have it any other way and I certainly had no objections. Now, from what you've told me, Sandquist, you weren't even in town that night and that can easily be proved. Karl Thorson claims that he wasn't in on it at all. In the event there is a conviction of all of you, we can appeal and have the whole thing thrown out. Everybody knows this, including the judge and the prosecutor. If ever there was a trial where the outcome wasn't in doubt, it is this one. But I'll let you in on a little secret. I am a personal friend of every member of the jury. Boys, relax. Have a nice lunch and I'll see you later. The one thing I want you to remember, is that you must never act like anything but the most perfect gentlemen in court. Lambert will not tolerate disrespect for the court. Now I saw a couple of you start to giggle at the old reprobate a little while ago. Well, don't. The judge doesn't like it. Just keep your mouth shut and let me do the talking for you."

Eight of the defendants got up to leave, but Karl held back. He wanted to talk to his defense attorney for reasons of his own. "Uh, Mr. Westgaard. Can I see you for a minute?"

"Sure, Karl, but I got an appointment for lunch so make it quick, will 'ya?"

"*Ja*. Well, I got another interest in this trial," Karl said, in a rather pathetic appeal.

"So I heard. And I saw you looking at Morrison's daughter all morning. Are you thinking I'm being too hard on her old man?"

"No, sir, it isn't that. But I wanted to have my story of what happened as part of the record so that she will know that I really did try to help out that night. You see, I was doing everything I could to stop the other guys. Sure, I admit that I hit Morrison with an egg, but that was just because I've got such lousy aim. I was

166

throwing at Rolf to prevent him from throwing at Morrison. The sheriff's report says that, I'm sure, and all the guys back me up. I know that I won't be convicted of anything, but I won't have won much if Julie still thinks that I attacked her father."

"Right. Well, I'll tell you what I'll do. I'll save that for the closing argument when I talk about all the other silly things in this case. See 'ya later." Westgaard dashed out the door and, after a quick look around, hopped in a car with three of the jury members.

Karl caught up with the other guys and they went downtown to the Bluebird Cafe for nine hot beef sandwiches and coffee. Paul was in an euphoric mood. "Sure beats plowing, huh Karl?"

15

The Verdict

15

Karl was looking in all of the cafe corners to see if Julie might just happen to be there. He wasn't at all sure that this did beat plowing. He finished his dinner long before the others.

Karl tried, without complete success, to listen to the story that Reidar had saved for just this moment. As the rest of the defendants leaned in to hear his story, Reidar took a sip of coffee and said, "*Ole*, he goes to the lawyer and he says 'I tink I want to get a divorce from *Lena*.' Well, the lawyer can hardly believe his ears and he says, 'You want to divorce *Lena*? Oh, *Ole*, I can't hardly believe that. What are the grounds?' Well, *Ole* looks at the lawyer like he can't figure out what he's talking about and he says, 'Vell, ve yust got da eighty acres.' So the lawyer, he says, 'No, *Ole*, that's not what I mean. Do you have a grudge?' And *Ole* he says 'Vell, sure. Ve got a grudge, but yew don't tink I'd let *Lena* put da Ford in dere all by herself, do yew?' So the lawyer thinks he better try something else and he says, 'Is *Lena* unfaithful, *Ole*?' and *Ole* tells him, 'Nei, she's a good Lutern.' Well, by this time the lawyer has just about run out of questions, but he tries one more. He says, '*Ole*, I hope you don't mind me getting too personal, but do you and *Lena* have mutual climax?' And *Ole* tells him, with a great deal of satisfaction, 'Nei, Ve got Lutern Brudderhood.' So the lawyer just says, 'I give up *Ole*. Just why is it that you want to divorce *Lena*?' And *Ole* tells him, 'Vel, she yust can't carry on an intelligent conversation!'"

Karl sat there as the conversation buzzed around him. Vaguely he heard Sigurd Nelson say, "Boy, you sure can tell old

171

Westgaard is a politician. He's a good guy, but like all the rest of them, he'll just get elected to raise our taxes."

To everyone's shock, Karl, who had taken virtually no part in the conversation, suddenly exploded. "Raise taxes! You damn right he should raise taxes. When are any of you ever going to learn that raising taxes is the best thing that can happen to us?"

While the rest sat in stunned disbelief Paul thought, "Oh God, here he goes again with the politics."

"Who do you guys think you are?" Karl demanded. "Andrew Mellon? Rockefeller? Carnegie? They are all good Republicans. They don't want their taxes raised. They can educate their own kids. Hell, they can buy their own universities. Which one of us can go to college? None of us! And the rich are going to make damn sure that we stay dumb so we won't compete with them."

"Now look," he continued, "the best way to tax is progressively. Those that have it pay a bigger percentage than those who don't, right? Right! But let's just take a straight percentage. Say the man who makes a million pays ten percent--same as the guy who makes a thousand. The millionaire pays a hundred thousand bucks in taxes, the other guys pays a hundred dollars. Yet they both get to go on the state highway, don't they? If we ever wake up, we can squeeze the fat cats who are squeezing the farmers. Sure, it would be nice to have ten or twelve bucks more at the end of the year. But by raising taxes, we can change society! And you guys who don't know sour owl shit about it, sit and bitch about nickels and dimes."

The outburst was not well received. While the rest turned back to their hot beef sandwiches in silence, Paul--in an all too rare show of understanding--said, "Hey, Karl, it's not our fault that Julie isn't here. Maybe you can see her after this is over."

The nine defendants were back in the courtroom in plenty time and were in their seats for twenty minutes before Westgaard showed up at one minute to two. He smiled at them and said, "Now don't forget to stand up when the judge comes into the room."

The words were hardly out of his mouth before the bailiff commanded them all to rise and Judge Lambert walked in looking as though he wished he were somewhere else.

As a somewhat surprise witness, Westgaard now called John Bunge to the stand. He was sworn to tell the truth and then immediately broke his oath by identifying his occupation as "projectionist." Everyone was content to let that pass, although it did produce a barely audible groan from the Vingelen crowd.

"Now then," said Westgaard, in an attempt to get right to the point, "will you describe your role in the showing of these films?"

"Sure. I was the projectionist," Bunge proudly allowed.

"Is that your regular occupation?"

"Well, it wasn't then. Morrison, he came to town and asked if anyone could run a movie projector and I figgered it couldn't be too difficult and so I sort of hinted that I could and he gave me the job."

"And what were your wages?"

"Huh?"

"Your wages. How much did he pay you for this?"

"Um, er, well, he didn't pay me anything. He said he was going to give me top projectionist wages of a dollar an hour, including the time it took to set things up and rewind the film. This was more than I had been making at the lumberyard so I thought that was a good deal. I figgered I had about six bucks coming from him but after that egg business, he left town and I never got paid. I tried to get ahold of him in Fargo, but he never answered my letter. I think I've been cheated!"

"Objection!" hollered the prosecution.

"Sustained," said the judge. "The jury will ignore the last statement of the witness."

Westgaard was content with the ruling and went on, "To continue, Mr. Bunge. Will you describe the types of films that you were showing those nights? I believe they were advertised as the 'latest films from Hollywood?'"

"*Ja*, that's what the posters said. Now, I admit that I don't know much about films and I've never been to Hollywood, but these films were not like any that I had ever seen. I showed five reels and they were all different and didn't go together at all. There was this cowboy movie and this Alaskan thing and then there was something about Florida and then the Keystone Kops. That was my favorite. I wish we could have had a few more reels about them. But then the last one was about these sword fighters in France. To tell you the truth, I'm not sure I showed them in the same order any of the nights, but it didn't seem to make any difference."

"And at any one of the showings, did you ever see a potential door prize of a live baby?"

"No."

"Did Morrison ever mention it?"

"No."

"Did you ever ask about it?"

"The first night, when he gave me the film cans, I asked him if he wanted to give the baby away between the reels or at the end. He just told me that he would take care of it and that I shouldn't worry about it."

"Thank you. No further questions."

And, since no one else had any questions for him, John Bunge stepped down and resumed his seat in the gallery. At this point, Westgaard called what could only be described as a surprise witness. A Dr. Harvey Boyle was asked to take the stand. Everyone looked puzzled as Dr. Boyle, who had an incredibly distinguished face partially obscured by a handlebar mustache, was sworn in.

"Now, Dr. Boyle. Will you please state your profession?"

"Yes. I am chairman of the department of biology at Moorhead State Teacher's College."

"What is your background for this position?"

"I have a Ph.D. degree in biological sciences from the University of Wisconsin, and have fourteen years of college teaching experience."

"Will you tell the court the age at which a rooster ceases to be a baby?"

"I'm not sure I want to get into the difference between a baby rooster--which we generally refer to as a chick, by the way--and an adolescent rooster. I can say, however, that a rooster reaches maturity in about six months."

"So an eleven-month-old rooster would hardly be a baby?"

174

"Hardly. A rooster might be able to live five or six years. He never does, of course, because he is usually in somebody's stewpot long before then, but in human terms, an eleven-month-old rooster would be comparable in age to the defendants in this case. If I may add, it is difficult to picture any of them in diapers."

"Thank you, Dr. Boyle. No further questions."

The crowded courtroom was roaring. The defendants tried to keep their demeanor, but most were failing. Judge Lambert had never spent a more absurd day in court and gave every appearance of wanting to get the trial over with as soon as possible. Karl, meanwhile, had been trying to catch Julie's eye ever since she had returned to the courtroom. As the crowd in the gallery laughed, the judge didn't even make a token effort to quiet them. Juliette Morrison covered her face with her hands and ran sobbing out of the courtroom. Karl knew that he could not follow her out, and felt certain that he would never see her again. Other than Morrison, he was the only person in the room who did not share in the hilarity of the moment.

Westgaard had one more witness to call. Johnny Bakken lumbered up to the stand and placed his pudgy hand on the Bible and swore to tell the truth (or at least his version of it).

"Now, Mr. Bakken. You are the constable of the Village of Vingelen?"

"*Ja.*"

"Were you on duty the night of August the 29th?"

"*Ja.*"

"You have informed the sheriff that you did not see any assault take place, nor did you see a cross burned. Is that correct?"

"Vell, I seen da fire, all right. But I vas up by da schoolhouse at dat time. Yew yust never know ven some kid vill decide to do someting to da school, yew know, and so I yust seen da glow from da fire. I couldn't tell dat it vas a cross. I hear day used some excelsior, and dat stuff burns purdy quick, yew know. By da time I got dere, dere vas nottin' but a few sparks left. I figgered it vas yust a bonfire of some kind and I didn't know nottin' about no cross 'til Morrison started telling me about it. Anyhow, I never seen no cross."

"What can you tell us about the local chapter of the Ku Klux Klan in Vingelen?"

"Huh? Dere ain't no Ku Klux Klan in Vingelen."

"Are you sure? It is a secret society, you know. It is called the 'Invisible Empire.'"

"Vell, by golly, it sure is invisible in Vingelen, den. I ain't never seen a single sheet in town dat ain't on a bed or a clothesline. I told Morrison at da time--told him I tought da boys were yust shittin' him a bit. Oh, ah, sorry, Your Honor. I mean dat dey were yust kiddin' him, yew know. Nobody in town would yoin an outfit like dat."

"Thank you, Mr. Bakken. No further questions."

As the Vingelen constable stepped down, Westgaard continued. "I will now place in evidence a deposition which I have obtained from a high-ranking member of the Fargo, North Dakota, chapter of the Ku Klux Klan. In it, he states that at no time has he or any other member of the Fargo chapter had any communication with anyone from Vingelen."

"Would the prosecutor like to examine this document?" asked Judge Lambert.

"Ah, no. That's all right. I'll take your word for it," replied the prosecutor, thinking that he would have been able to provide a better defense for John Wilkes Booth.

Johnny Bakken was the last witness. The prosecutor stepped forward to make his closing arguments to the jury.

"Gentlemen of the jury. The prosecution will concede that there was no Ku Klux Klan in Vingelen on the evening of the 29th of August. We will also concede that the advertisements for the door prize to be given away at the conclusion of the film series may have been misleading. But, and this is a big but, (the prosecutor--who was given to increasing obesity--inwardly cringed when he realized what he had just said), Mr. Morrison is not on trial here. We have definitely established that Mr. Morrison was cruelly assaulted with rotten eggs and that at least one of these eggs caused bodily harm. Although the Klan may not have been genuine in Vingelen, Mr. Morrison could not know that and the effect of the prank was a deliberate act of terror. Laws have been broken here, and you can't change that fact by pointing out the ridiculousness of Mr. Morrison, I mean, by trying to make Mr. Morrison appear ridiculous. The laws of the State of Minnesota are sacred, and justice will not be served by acquitting young men who have openly acted illegally. I urge a conviction!" (And I strongly hope you won't listen to me or I'm done in this county, thought the prosecutor to himself.)

Westgaard solemnly approached the jury, breathed deeply, and put on his best vote-getting manner.

"Gentlemen, we have here a case that never should have come to trial. The testimony has established that the whole community was a victim of a confidence scheme. The use of a tiny baby, a creation of God, to sell tickets to a moving picture show is such a disgusting practice that most communities would not have been blamed for throwing eggs *before* the films ever started. Then, to insult this community of agricultural experts– yeoman farmers who produce the food that sustains us all– by trying to pass off an eleven-month-old rooster as a baby... well, words fail me!" (If so, it would have been the first time in his career.)

"Had the charge been a misdemeanor, such as disorderly conduct, these boys might have pled guilty if only to show their respect for the laws of the great State of Minnesota. But that was not charged. They were charged with assault and battery. Do any of you really believe that such a fine collection of young men from our very own county, could be capable of such a thing?"

"No! No! No! Of course not! Not only that, but we can prove that one of the young men on trial here was not even in Vingelen on the night of August 29th, thus proving that Mr. Morrison's recollection of the events of that night are fuzzy at best, perjury at worst. Furthermore, I have one more example of the fine character of these boys. While others in the crowd were playfully throwing eggs at a man who had attempted, and in many cases had succeeded, to defraud the public, Mr. Karl Thorson was attempting to stop it."

Morrison, who had been staring at the floor, suddenly looked up in astonishment. He cranked his neck to see the embarrassed Karl now looking at the floor. What good does this do now, Karl thought. Julie isn't even here anymore.

"Yes. Karl Thorson threw an egg that struck Mr. Morrison on the back of the head, causing him to lose his balance and fall into a telephone pole. But Mr. Thorson was attempting to stop another person from attacking Mr. Morrison. It is no fault of Mr. Thorson that he is not a blessed athlete. He missed. But for this gallant action, he was rewarded with an arrest warrant for assault and battery. I know that justice will be served here, and I know that you will return a verdict of 'Not Guilty.' Thank you, gentlemen."

The gallery broke into spontaneous applause which Westgaard deftly acknowledged by a slight nod of his head. Judge Lambert looked sourly at the clock and gavelled the crowd into silence. His instructions to the jury were a model of clarity, efficiency, and expediency.

"Gentlemen of the jury. If you find the defendants guilty as charged, they face a prison sentence for the serious crime of assault and battery. If you do not, they do not. Please retire to the deliberating room and return as soon as you have reached a verdict."

Judge Lambert was sure that when the jury went into the room, they would almost meet themselves coming back out.

It was now almost four o'clock. He had a bottle of very elderly Canadian whiskey in his chambers that he had picked up the last time he was in Winnipeg. He thought he would be magnanimous and offer that poor sap of a prosecutor a snort to cheer him up. He decided to go to his chambers and get a start on the bottle and they could call him when the jury was ready.

Meanwhile, Karl and the rest of the defendants were also starting to get uneasy. Karl finally caught the eye of Westgaard as he was doing a little politicking in the corner of the courtroom.

"What's taking them so long?" asked Karl anxiously. "I thought you said everything was all fixed."

"Yeah, still nothing to worry about. I just got a hunch about those guys on the jury. You see, if their deliberations go beyond the supper hour, the county has to buy them a meal. I think they they are just waiting around for a free supper."

Nevertheless, Karl still felt worried about the outcome. There

178

was, after all, a point in what the prosecutor had said; they had broken some kind of law. Karl, therefore, stationed himself outside the deliberating room. A short time later, one of the jury members came out and whispered to the bailiff that he had to go to the restroom. As he opened the door, billows of cigar smoke came out and Karl was able to see six poker hands dealt out. It seemed that justice in Minnesota was in good hands after all.

At six o'clock, six dinners were brought into the deliberating room. At six-thirty, the bailiff reported that the jury had reached a decision. The crowd, or at least that which was left of it, hurried back into the courtroom. Many from the Vingelen area had had to rush home to do the chores, and Karl and Paul were sort of secretly enjoying the fact that Pa was stuck doing their chores. The jury looked to be in a good mood, especially the winners of the last two hands.

Belatedly, Judge Lambert came in. He was as drunk as a lord, but he knew it and tried to over-compensate for his infirmity. He gripped the rail tightly the whole way to the bench and sat down as quickly as he could.

"Gentlemen of the jury. Have you in your solemn duty reached a verdict?" intoned the judge, who was looking curiously pale.

"We have, Your Honor."

Several moments of embarrassing silence followed.

"Well, damnit. What is it?"

"Oh, sorry. Not Guilty, of course."

"Good for you!" Judge Lambert roared as he stood up and then immediately fell down.

16

An Ending and Perhaps a Beginning

16

One more round to go. One more pass down the quarter mile length of the field and a quarter mile back again. Plowing would soon be over for the year of 1926.

It was late October. It had already snowed once, but a short Indian summer had taken care of that. It was now cold again. Karl wore two pairs of pants and two pairs of socks and he was still chilled to the bone. Depressing dark clouds hung low over the fields and made the day seem even shorter than it was.

There is something morbid about misty late October days in Minnesota. Color and warmth have disappeared from the earth. The acres of black plowed fields are distinguised only by a muddy road, a thin weedy property line, a barbed wire fence, or a line of trees. The trees acquire a sameness, for even though their shapes may be different, their rain-blackened limbs adopt a uniform color, rather like the grey-black granite tombstones at the Småland Lutheran Church. For some reason, even the cows seem depressed on days like this. They lie in silence stoically enduring the chill, with their once lush pastures now brown with only occasional frost-killed thistles remaining.

Some people loved days like this. Karl marveled at how his friends could enthusiastically rant on about hiding in a duck blind to blast some ducks. He had once interrupted a hunting story to point out how chicken was tastier than duck, easier to acquire, and when one figured in the costs of shooting the unfortunate duck, a whole lot cheaper per pound. The narrator of the duck story, and each of his avid listeners, looked at Karl as though he were the worst sort of heretic. Karl could never understand why anyone would enjoy sitting in a cold slough. He had no great humanitarian concern about ducks, but he could not see the fun in waiting all day to take the life of another creature. He did get perverse enjoyment out of the hunting activities of Paul and Pa, however for when they were out hunting, he sat by the stove, sipping hot coffee, and reading a tale of the sea.

Karl dropped the plow down into the moist furrow and let the powerful Twin City 17-28 finish the autumn chores. He remembered Pa's first tractor, a Bull Tractor, "the Bull with the Pull". With the Bull, Karl had to sit on the plow while Pa drove the tractor. It was Karl's duty to take the plow out of the ground at the end of the field and drop it in at the start of the next round. It was dangerous work because whenever the plow struck a rock, he would bounce a foot or two up in the air. He would come down on the plow frame and his feet would come close to the rolling colters that sliced deeply into the earth. He had hated that job and he would never forget the Bull.

Plowing offered a great time to think. Karl would drop the plow into the ground, take a few clods of dirt off the steel tractor wheels and amuse himself by throwing the clods at any sea gull that came within range. Sometimes his aim was not too bad. Oh, he thought, if only he could have thrown as well when he tried to keep Rolf from hitting Doc Morrison.

He had never seen Julie again. He had gone to Fargo to find the place where she had been staying. The only information they could give him was that Morrison and his daughter had moved to somewhere in the Twin Cities. That took in a lot of territory!

Meanwhile, things quickly settled down in Vingelen. Pa was busier than ever at the elevator because they had also taken over the new potato house that had been built just to the south, and the potato crop was the best in years. As usual, the Vingelen Consolidated School was let out for two weeks so pupils could help with the potato picking. For some children it meant the chance to earn enough money for a whole year's worth of school clothes, and for their parents it was an economic necessity.

Pa was doing quite well, but it meant that Karl was busier than

184

ever on the farm. Paul was not much help. The owner of the Vingelen Garage had suffered a mild heart attack and had asked Paul to take over the garage for him until he recovered. Does Paul care how much work I have to do on the farm? Apparently not! But at least he comes home in time to help with the chores. Anyway, with the plowing done, I guess I haven't really got all that much to do. Maybe I can get up to the Moorhead Library one of these days. There are a lot of books coming out about the Great War that I want to read. The way some of those guys came home, I'm glad that I was too young to go. Still, it would have been interesting to see Paris. Wonder if I'll ever get there?

Karl lifted the plow out of the ground, turned around, and began the last trip down the field.

I gotta do something with my life, he thought. I can't work Pa's farm all my life. If old man Nyhus decides to retire, maybe I could take over his farm. It's not worth much and he will have a hard time getting someone to rent it these days. Hard to think that it was one of the first farms ever settled around here. Pa said it used to be one of those 'bonanza' farms in the eighties. Huh, wish I could have seen it then. Pa said there even used to be a tunnel from the house to the barn. That would be something. I could marry Julie and we could rebuild the 'bonanza.' Ah, what am I thinking about that for? She'll never see me again, even if I do find out where she's gone.

If I start farming on my own, I sure would like to settle down with a wife and maybe have a couple of kids. There must be somebody around here I could start taking out. I suppose I could always do like Reidar and take some high school girl out. Nah, I don't want to do that. Karl came to the end of another year's plowing and, still deeply in thought, he guided the big tractor home.

There's the spot where I buried old Prince, thought Karl, as he made a wide detour around the semi-hallowed ground. *Fa'n*, but I hated that dog! Prince, in fact, had haunted Karl even after the dog's death. He had been one of the worst hunting dogs in the history of dogdom and one afternoon, after Prince had scared every pheasant in the township out of range of Pa's shotgun, Pa had used the old twelve gauge on poor Prince. The dead dog laid in the warm autumn sun for three days before Pa ordered Karl, only eleven years old, to bury the poor beast. Karl had been afraid of Prince while he was alive, and now he was terrified of him in death. He dug a deep hole several yards from the dog's body and slowly crept up and looped a long length of twine around the dog's hind foot. He extended the twine as far as it would go and then got on the other end to drag the bloated carcass to the hole. Then, in a mad fit of courage, Karl had rushed forward to pile dirt on him. After the dog was finally covered with a thin layer of earth, the rest of the job held no great terror. However, just then, the weight of the newly turned earth forced the air out of Prince and as it passed through the dog's throat a long mournful howl emerged. Karl had never been so scared in his life! He threw the spade over his shoulder and ran for the house and literally leapt into Ma's arms. Karl didn't return to the spot for several years and now, as he drove the tractor in a wide arc around Prince's immortal remains, he still felt a chill. Gosh, Karl thought, I'd rather go back to court than have to go through that again.

Karl's thoughts floated back to his most troublesome question; What to do with my life? Other guys my age have had a chance to go to college. They're starting a career and a family. Not me. Oh, what should I do with my life?

Perhaps the best thing about driving a tractor was that you did not have take off harnesses, curry, water or feed it. When you were done with it, you were done with it. Karl unhitched the plow halfway into the woods. There would be no need for it for several months. He parked the tractor under a cottonwood tree and put a tin can over the exhaust pipe. It was starting to get dark, and although a cup of coffee would really hit the spot and warm him up, it was now getting on to chores time. Karl felt that he should somehow be elated that fieldwork was over for the year, but as he ambled out to get the cows for milking, he felt depressed and lonely. There was really nothing to look forward to except winter and who, in their right mind, would look forward to winter in Minnesota?

"Commmmmmme, Boss. Commmmmmme, Boss. Here Bossy, Bossy, Bossy," he bellowed. Then a more pleasant thought struck him. He would soon have to choose one of those beasts to butcher. That was one great thing about living on the farm--he never had to worry where his next meal was coming from.

Soon it would be Thanksgiving. And then Christmas! Ah, he could see it now. Christmas Eve! *Lefse*. Ah, *lefse*! The Norwegian napkin! How could ordinary mashed potatoes and lard be rolled so thin and yet taste so good? He loved it best hot off the griddle with only butter, but it was also great when it was all rolled up with sugar. And then there would be *lutefisk, lutefisk* in rich cream sauce. How could those pure Norwegians choke it down with just drawn butter? And, there would also be *krumkaker, fattigmann, sandbakkler,* potato sausage, *julekake,* some imported *sild,* sweet soup, and maybe-- best of all-- *rømmegrøt.* Oh yeah, life was worth living as long as there was Christmas and Ma was free to practice her greatest art!

Christmas was always a fun time because that was when people went *julebukking.* Karl wondered if *julebukking* was a Norwegian word or a Swedish word: Oh well, most people are starting to call it 'Christmas fooling' anyhow. I wonder what kind of get-up I can invent this year? Indeed, it was something to look forward to. Everyone would disguise themselves and go to someone else's farmhouse. The fortunate and often randomly chosen surprised host was prevailed upon to guess the identity of his guests. A failure to do so meant that he had to provide a treat which, if they were lucky, might be a glass of wine or even something a little more illegal. Most of the visits, however, resulted in coffee and Christmas cookies. A successful guess of the disguised person, however, usually brought the same reward so it didn't really matter much, and the hosts often joined the *julebukkers* as they went on to the next farmhouse. Still, the more Karl though about it, the more he began to be depressed again. Most of the *julebukking* was now done in couples. It would be another lonely Christmas.

Ma came in and Karl made small talk with her about how nice it was to be done with the plowing for another year. Finally, Paul came home from town and joined them in the barn.

"Hey, Karl," said Paul with kindness that had grown since the

Morrison debacle, "I see you got done with the plowing. Why don't you go in and wash up. I'll take over here. Looks like Ma's got a pretty good start on the milking already."

Karl mumbled his thanks and took him up on the suggestion. He slowly walked into the house and removed the various layers of clothes. He washed his face, neck, and his arms up to his elbows. He sat down by the stove and began to peruse a copy of the **Decorah Posten**. Since it was printed in Norwegian, Karl usually didn't read too much of it, but he did love the *Ola and Per* cartoons of Peter Rosendahl. Ma, who was, after all, Norwegian, read it religiously and was especially devoted to the *Hjemme och Kvinna*, or the "Home and Woman" section. He hadn't read very much before Pa walked in.

"Hi, Pa. You buy a lot of potatoes today?" said Karl, barely looking up from his newspaper.

"*Nei*, I tink dat's yust about over for da year too. I noticed da plow vas shoved into da voods. Finished her up, heh?"

"*Ja*. Done for another year, I guess."

"Ma and Paul still down in da barn?"

"*Ja*."

"Den I got something I vant to talk over wit yew."

Pa slowly settled himself in a wooden chair across from Karl and after a weighty pause began, "Yew know, tings have been purty good at the elevator dis year. Dat new spud house has kept me awful busy lately. Vell, da elevator board, dey got tegetter today, an dey figger it's time dey got somebody full-time to run dat ting. So dey talked it over and dey asked me if I vould vant to be da full-time manager. Vell, yew know, my back has been gettin' vorse and vorse every year, and I ben wondering yust how long I can keep dis here farming up, yew know. So I tink maybe Ma and I vill move to town and I'll do da elevator ting for a vile and I vas vondering if maybe yew vould like to, yew know, take over da farm?"

Karl was stunned. Somehow the thought that he would be able to take over Pa's farm in the near future had really not occurred to him. But now,... now it was perfect. He anxiously replied, "Well, sure. *Ja*. I'd like that very much. But what about

Paul?"

"Vell, yew know I already talked to him about it. Ve vere out duck hunting last Sunday morning. I knew dere vas dis shanse I'd be offered da elevator yob and so I asks him how he felt about it and if he vould like to farm wit yew. I tink it made him feel a little funny, but he says dat, no, he really tinks he likes vot he's doing vorking in dat garage and he figgers he'd ratter do dat den farm. He said he'd like to stay on here for a vile and help yew out, but dat he ain't gonna farm all his life, yew see?"

The fire in the stove crackled. The heat seemed intense. Karl leaned forward with his elbows on his knees and his face in his hands. He thought, so that's it. The future comes not through my work or my dreams or my plans, but just drops from the sky. Nobody looks up and tells you to jump. You do the best you can and maybe things fall in your lap; maybe they don't. So that's it, then. I'm gonna be a good farmer. I'm gonna be a damn good farmer.

He looked up to see Pa anxiously watching him and said, "I don't know when I could start to pay you for it."

"Ah, who cares about dat? Ve'll vork someting out. Da prices are so lousy now days so's I don't tink yew could do it if yew tried. But yew know, it means someting to me, and it means someting to Ma, too, to be able to leave dis here farm in your hands. Yew vill be a better farmer den I ever vas, I tink."

Karl felt kind of strange. He remained silent for a moment, but as his father slowly rose with a prolonged wheeze he, too, stood up. He rather abruptly put his arm around his father's shoulder, realized how much he had always loved him, and said with sort of a choked gasp, "Thanks, Pa......er, Daddy."

This was more than Pa could take. He turned away and mumbled something about going to see what was taking so long "down da barn", and began walking to the door. Then he abruptly turned.

"Oh, by da vay. I stopped by da post office to see if ve got any mail. Dis heres for yew."

Karl looked down at the letter. The return address read: "J. Morrison. 1421 Franklin Avenue, Minneapolis, Minnesota." It was Julie! Karl decided to read it in the privacy of his own room.

He carried a lamp up the stairs and set it on the nightstand. He sat down on the bed and became aware that his hands were getting the envelope all sweaty and he was sure that he could hear his own heartbeat. He allowed a full minute to go by before he carefully opened the envelope and took out three thin, blue pieces of stationery. The letter read:

Dear Karl,

I know I should have written sooner, but I was just too ashamed of myself. I should have known that you would not have been a part of what was done to my father. I do so apologize for having doubted you, and I hope you can forgive me. I left the courtroom before your attorney explained how you had actually tried to protect my father. I wish that I had stayed longer and had heard it myself because then I could have apologized to you in person. As it was, I didn't find out about your part in it until the next day. After the trial, my father was quite upset.

We left on the train for Minneapolis the very next morning. We finally had a long talk on the train. Perhaps it was sitting next to each other for five hours or something but, in any event, we talked to each other on that day more than at any time since my mother died. He told me that the testimony at the trial brought out your side of what happened and went so far as to say that you must be a fine young man indeed to stand up to friends in such a manner. On this at least, my father and I agree completely.

Ironically, it seems some good may have come from all this. My father now admits that his venture into the movie business was nothing but a calculated swindle, but he is also convinced that the motion picture industry holds a lot of promise. He was able to get a job managing one of the larger moving picture theaters in Minneapolis by somewhat overstating his experience in Vingelen. He likes what he is doing, and at last may be on the verge of a stable career.

It might surprise you to learn I have become somewhat of a farmer myself. After some searching, I was able to get a job at Forbes Nursery on Lyndale Avenue. I was hired to be a sales girl in the flower shop but after only one day on the job, I was moved out to work in the hot house. The man who usually did that job hurt his back but naturally, he wanted to keep working. So, Mr. Forbes gave him my job. Well, I wanted to work too, so Mr. Forbes said I could try to take over the hot house work. Today I spent most of the morning spreading horse manure on flower beds. And you know I even liked that, smell and all. It is really exciting to plant something yourself and then see it come up and start to grow. I think I can appreciate the satisfaction that you get from farming.

I've also been reading a book that seems like the kind of book that you would enjoy. It's called **Lord *Jim*** by Joseph Conrad. It's about this sea captain who is responsible for the lives of hundreds of people and in a storm, he abandons his ship and then has to live with his decision. We didn't have much of a chance to talk about this kind of thing, but you seem to have read a lot. Reading is the one activity that kept me entertained during those long nights in all those small town hotels.

At present we are renting the whole upstairs of a nice house on Franklin Avenue within walking distance of Father's theater. He is at last keeping regular hours. I don't know what was in that egg you hit him with, but it sure worked!

I remember hearing that the Vingelen basketball team often comes down to St. Paul for the state tournaments. (Isn't it time one of those Schmidt brothers graduates from high school?) I will go to the tournament this year and cheer for Vingelen because, even though it was the town that threw eggs at my father, it is the town of the most honorable young man I have ever met. Perhaps I will even see you there.

In the meantime, if you ever happen to come down to the cities, be sure and stop by.

With deepest regards,
Julie

P.S. I know you were one of the guys who pushed that wagon into the lake, and I don't mind at all.

Karl held the letter and stared at the wall. The rose pattern of the wallpaper went out of focus and the pink flowers seemed to hover a few inches in front of the tan background. Half an hour ago he had dragged himself in from the fields and put his future to rest with the same finality with which he put the tin can on the exhaust pipe of the tractor. But now a profound, almost delirious, happiness enveloped him--a happiness that was too grand to keep to himself yet, in its magnitude, impossible to share. It was an all-consuming happiness that seemed to flow from his mind through his muscles and into his bones to the tips of the fingers that held Julie's letter. After a few uncountable minutes he became aware that his face actually hurt from smiling.

It was in such a state that Paul found him. Paul had shared his brother's agony over his lost love and had felt a certain measure of responsibility for it. Now, mirroring Karl's smile, he said, "Pa said you got a letter. I hope it's from Julie."

Dimly, from out of the recesses of Karl's memory came the words that Pastor Lindstrom had read from the fifth chapter of Romans on that summer Sunday before the egg fight, "Endurance produces character, character produces hope, and hope does not disappoint us."

ORDER FORM
for
Uffda Trial

Name _____

Address _____

City _____ State _____ Zip _____

No. of copies _____ @ $9.95 **Subtotal** $ _____

Plus postage & handling (per book)

      1st Class $3.00 per book $ _____

      Book Rate $1.50 per book $ _____

(Maximum postage cost for multiple orders: $6.00)

MN Residents add 6.5% Sales Tax $ _____

                  TOTAL: $ _____

Send cash, check or money order to:
MARTIN HOUSE PUBLICATIONS
P.O. BOX 274
HASTINGS, MN 55033

OTHER BOOKS AND PRODUCTS published by Janet
Martin and Martin House Publications:

- Cream Peas On Toast
- They Glorified Mary/We Glorified Rice
- They Had Stores/We Had Chores
- Lutheran Church Basement Women & Dishtowel
- Shirley Holmquist and Aunt Wilma Who Dunit?
- Second Helpings of Cream & Bread
- Cream & Bread
- Helga Hanson Hotflash Hankies

For copies write to: Martin House Publications,
                     P.O. Box 274, Hastings, MN 55033
                     or call 1-800-950-6898